Why Read Hannah Arendt Now

For Jerry Kohn

Why Read
Hannah Arendt Now

Richard J. Bernstein

polity

First published in 2018 by Polity Press

10

Polity Press
65 Bridge Street
Cambridge CB2 1UR, UK

Polity Press
101 Station Landing
Suite 300
Medford, MA 02155, USA

ISBN-13: 978-1-5095-2859-2
ISBN-13: 978-1-5095-2860-8(pb)

A catalogue record for this book is available from the British Library.

Library of Congress Cataloging-in-Publication Data
Names: Bernstein, Richard J., author.
Title: Why read Hannah Arendt now / Richard Bernstein.
Description: Cambridge ; Medford, MA : Polity Press, 2018. | Includes bibliographical references and index. |
Identifiers: LCCN 2017050361 (print) | LCCN 2018002934 (ebook) | ISBN 9781509528639 (Epub) | ISBN 9781509528592 (hardback) | ISBN 9781509528608 (pbk.)
Subjects: LCSH: Arendt, Hannah, 1906-1975--Criticism and interpretation. | Arendt, Hannah, 1906-1975--Political and social views.
Classification: LCC JC251.A74 (ebook) | LCC JC251.A74 B47 2018 (print) | DDC 320.5--dc23
LC record available at https://lccn.loc.gov/2017050361

Typeset in 12.5 on 15 pt Adobe Garamond by
Servis Filmsetting Ltd, Stockport, Cheshire
Printed and bound in Great Britain by TJ Books Limited

For further information on Polity, visit our website:
politybooks.com

Contents

Acknowledgments

I have dedicated this book to Jerry (Jerome) Kohn, a friend for more than twenty-five years. Jerry has done more than anyone else to make Hannah Arendt known to the international public. He has been a judicious editor of her published and unpublished works. His own writings on Arendt are always perceptive and illuminating. He has been an inspiration in my own journey with Arendt. I want to thank Professor Carol Bernstein for reading and editing my manuscript. She is, without doubt, my toughest and most incisive critic. Caecilie Varslev-Petersen helped to prepare this book for publication. Once again, I want to express my gratitude to Jean van

Altena, who has skillfully edited my manuscript. John Thompson, who suggested that I write this book, has always been a source of encouragement.

Introduction

When Hannah Arendt died in December 1975, she was known primarily because of the controversy about her report on the trial of Adolf Eichmann and the phrase "the banality of evil." There was a circle of admirers and critics in the United States and in Germany who were knowledgeable about her other writings, but she was scarcely considered to be a major political thinker. In the years since her death the scene has changed radically. Her books have been translated into dozens of languages. All over the world, people are passionately interested in her work. There seems to be no end of books, conferences, and articles focusing on Arendt and her ideas. Recently discussions and references to Arendt have overflowed social media. Why this growing interest – and why especially the recent spike of interest in her work? Arendt was remarkably perceptive about some of the deepest problems, perplexities, and dangerous tendencies in modern political life. Many of these have not disappeared; they have become more intense and more dangerous. When Arendt spoke about "dark times" she was not exclusively referring to the horrors of twentieth-century totalitarianism. She writes:

> If it is the function of the public realm to throw light on the affairs of men by providing a space of appearances in which they can show in deed and word, for better or worse, who they are and what they can do, then darkness has come when this light is extinguished by "credibility gaps" and "invisible government," by speech that does not disclose what is but sweeps it under the carpet, by exhortations, moral and otherwise, that, under the pretext of upholding old truths, degrade all truth in meaningless triviality. (Arendt 1968: p. viii)[1]

It is hard to resist the conclusion that we are now living in dark times that are engulfing the entire world. Arendt claims that even in the darkest of times we can hope to find some illumination – illumination that comes not so much from theories and concepts but from the lives and works of individuals. I want to show

1 Arendt consistently used masculine nouns and pronouns to refer to human beings. For stylistic purposes, I have followed her practice.

that Arendt provides such illumination, that she helps us to gain critical perspective on our current political problems and perplexities. She is an astute critic of dangerous tendencies in modern life and she illuminates the potentialities for restoring the dignity of politics. This is why she is worth reading and rereading today.

But who was Hannah Arendt? I will begin with a brief sketch of some of the highlights of her life that shaped her thinking. She was drawn to Machiavelli's appeal to the goddess *Fortuna* (roughly translated as "luck," "chance," "contingency"). Luck, as we know, can be good or bad. Unlike her close friend, Walter Benjamin, who always seemed to experience bad luck and finally committed suicide, Arendt's *Fortuna* was favorable at crucial moments in her life. Born in 1906 into a German–Jewish secular family she became an outstanding member of a gifted generation of German–Jewish intellectuals. In the early 1920s she studied with Germany's outstanding philosophers and theologians, including Husserl, Heidegger, Jaspers, and Bultmann. With the ominous growth of the Nazis and their rabid antisemitism, Arendt agreed to help her Zionist friends by doing research on Nazi antisemitic propaganda. In 1933 she was apprehended and interrogated for eight days. She refused to reveal what she was doing but was finally released. This was an extraordinary piece of good luck because we know that many others in similar circumstances were murdered in the cellars of the Gestapo.

Arendt then decided to leave Germany illegally. She escaped through Czechoslovakia and made her way to Paris – the refuge for many Jews fleeing from the Nazis. Arendt was officially stateless for eighteen years until she became an American citizen. This is a primary reason for her sensitivity to the plight of the stateless and to the troubled status of refugees. Illegal German exiles in Paris faced the problem of not having official papers permitting them to work, so many led extremely precarious lives. Arendt had the good fortune to secure employment with several Jewish and Zionist organizations, including Youth Aliyah – the organization that sent endangered European Jewish youths to Palestine. In Paris she met Heinrich Blücher, who came from a German gentile family, had participated in the Spartacist uprising, and had been a member of the German Communist Party. They were married in 1940. In

4

May 1940, shortly before the Germans invaded France, French authorities ordered all "enemy aliens" between the ages of seventeen and fifty-five to be sent to internment camps. Arendt was sent to Gurs, a camp in southern France near the Spanish border. In an article written shortly after Arendt arrived in New York, she ironically refers to a new kind of human being created by contemporary history – "the kind that are put in concentration camps by their foes and in internment camps by their friends" (Arendt 2007: 265). Arendt managed to escape from Gurs during the brief period when the Nazis invaded France. Many of the women who did not escape were eventually sent to Auschwitz on the orders of Adolf Eichmann. Arendt had been separated from Heinrich and her mother when she was interned. She was lucky again because she managed to be reunited with them – once again by a series of fortunate accidents.

Now the challenge became how to escape from Europe as a stateless illegal German–Jewish refugee. The problem was twofold: how to get a visa for the United States, and how to get out of France and travel to Portugal to take a ship to New York. There are disturbing parallels between the Kafkaesque difficulties that European Jews experienced and the horrendous obstacles that Syrian Muslim refugees now confront in seeking legal entry into the United States. In each instance, there has been enormous suspicion and hostility directed toward these refugees and excessively severe visa restrictions. *Fortuna* (almost as if Arendt was protected by the goddess) intervened again. Hannah and Heinrich were able to secure visas from Varian Fry who headed the Emergency Rescue Committee in Marseille. They managed to avoid the French police who were searching for them, succeeded in escaping from France, traveled across Spain, and arrived in Lisbon where they waited three months for a ship to take them to the United States. In May 1941 Arendt and her husband arrived in New York. Hannah's mother arrived a month later.

Retrospectively, we can see how lucky Arendt was, how chance events meant the difference between life and death. She might have been murdered in Berlin when she was interrogated. She might have failed to escape from Gurs and eventually been sent to Auschwitz. She might have failed to get a visa and, like so many Jews

stranded in France, been sent to a German concentration camp. Arendt arrived in New York
at the age of thirty-five barely knowing any
English. Her mother tongue was German and
she always loved the German language, especially
German poetry. Before 1941 she had never been
in an English-speaking country. Nevertheless,
Arendt set out to master English. Assisted by
friends who helped to "English" her writings, she
started publishing articles in local Jewish periodi-
cals. She found work with Jewish organizations,
including the Commission on European Jewish
Cultural Reconstruction, and she secured a position as a senior editor at Schocken Books.

In 1944 she submitted a proposal to Houghton
Mifflin Press for a book that she proposed to
write. She called it "The Elements of Shame: Anti-
Semitism – Imperialism – Racism." She spent the
next four years intensively working on her book.
She changed her mind several times about its
scope and contents. Relatively late in the process
of writing she decided to change the focus and
deal with totalitarianism. In 1951 *The Origins of
Totalitarianism*, a book of more than 500 densely
written pages, was published. In its final form
it consisted of three major parts: Antisemitism,

Imperialism, Totalitarianism. *The Origins* was immediately recognized as a major contribution to the study of totalitarianism. Actually, the title is misleading because one might be led to believe that Arendt is giving a historical account of the origins and causes of totalitarianism in the twentieth century. But Arendt's project is quite different. She set out to trace the disparate "subterranean elements" that "crystallized" in the horrible originality of totalitarianism. As with all her major writings the reception of *The Origins* was controversial – and still is. Nevertheless, it established her as a major political thinker. For the next twenty-five years Arendt continued to publish provocative books and collections of essays, including *The Human Condition, Rahel Varnhagen, Between Past and Future, Eichmann in Jerusalem, On Revolution, Men in Dark Times, On Violence, Crises of the Republic*, and (posthumously) *The Life of the Mind.* Since her death, many of her unpublished manuscripts have been published and continue to be published. I do not plan to give a survey of her work. Rather, I will concentrate on a set of central themes that are relevant to problems and perplexities that we are facing today. I want to show why we should read

Hannah Arendt today – how her life and work illuminate the current dark times.

Statelessness and Refugees

> I have always believed that, no matter how abstract our theories may sound or how consistent our arguments may appear, there are incidents and stories behind them which at least for ourselves, contain in a nutshell the full meaning of whatever we have to say. Thought itself – to the extent that it is more than a technical, logical operation which electronic machines may be better equipped to perform than the human brain – arises out of the actuality of incidents, and incidents of living experience must remain its guideposts by which thinking soars, or into the depths to which it descends. (Arendt 2018: 200–1)

This passage reveals a profound characteristic of Arendt as a thinker. She believed that serious thinking should be grounded in one's lived experience. Arendt's primary experience from the time that she escaped Germany, fled France, and arrived in New York was as a stateless German–Jewish refugee. If Arendt had not been aided by refugee organizations, she would not have received a visa or the financial aid to travel to the United States. When she arrived in New York, she was modestly assisted by refugee organizations in getting settled. Throughout her life, many of Arendt's closest friends were also refugees who had fled from the Nazis. Her lived experience as a stateless refugee shaped her earliest thinking in Paris and New York. Arendt tells us that, as a child, she was barely aware of her Jewishness. But during the 1920s she became aware of the viciousness of Nazi antisemitism. In an interview reflecting on this period of her life she writes: "I realized what I then expressed time and time again in the sentence: If one is attacked as a Jew, one must defend oneself as a Jew. Not as a German, not as a world citizen, not as an upholder of the Rights of Man, or whatever" (Arendt 1994: 11–12).

During the 1930s and 1940s most of her writings dealt with various aspects of the Jewish Question and Zionism. She became a regular columnist for the German-Jewish newspaper *Aufbau*, published in New York and read primarily by other German–Jewish exiles. She argued fervently for the creation of an international Jewish army to fight Hitler – even before the

United States entered into the Second World War. In 1943, just two years after her arrival in New York, she published "We Refugees" in an obscure Jewish journal. She wrote about refugees with insight, wit, irony, and a deep sense of melancholy. She opens her article by declaring: "In the first place, we don't like to be called 'refugees.' We ourselves call each other 'newcomers' or 'immigrants'" (Arendt 2007: 264). At one time a refugee was a person driven to seek refuge because of some act committed or some political opinion held. But this has now changed because most of those who fled never dreamed of holding radical opinions. Arendt declares that we were forced to become refugees not because of anything we did or said, but because the Nazis condemned all of us as members of the Jewish race. "With us the meaning of the term 'refugee' had changed. Now 'refugees' are those of us who have been so unfortunate as to arrive in a new country without means and have to be helped by refugee committees" (Arendt 2007: 264). Many refugees professed to be optimistic, hoping to build new lives in a new country. Mocking the absurdities of the aspiration to adjust rapidly and assimilate to a new country, Arendt tells the story of the German

Jew who, having arrived in France, "founded one of these societies of adjustment in which German Jews asserted to each other that they were already Frenchmen. In his first speech, he said: 'We have been good Germans in Germany and therefore we shall be good Frenchmen in France.' The public applauded enthusiastically and nobody laughed; we were happy to have learned how to prove our loyalty" (Arendt 2007: 272). But the sad truth, Arendt claimed, was that we lost our homes, we lost our occupations, and we lost our language. We lost many of our family and friends who had been killed in concentration camps. We were given "friendly advice" to forget and not talk about past horrors. Nobody wants to hear about that. But there was something superficial and false about this professed optimism. Such optimism could easily turn into speechless pessimism – and some of us even turned on the gas and committed suicide.

Arendt knew that she was speaking about unpopular facts. She felt that behind the facade of optimistic cheerfulness there was a constant struggle with despair and a deep confusion about identity. Arendt was always far more independent than many of her fellow refugees, but she wrote:

The less we are free to decide who we are or to live as we like, the more we try to put up a front, to hide the facts, and to play roles. We were expelled from Germany because we were Jews. But having hardly crossed the French borderline, we were changed into *boches* [French slang for Germans – RJB]. We were even told that we had to accept this designation if we really were against Hitler's racial theories. During seven years we played the ridiculous role of trying to be Frenchmen – at least, prospective citizens; but at the beginning of the war we were interned as *boches* all the same. In the meantime, however, most of us had become such loyal Frenchmen that we could not even criticize a French government order; thus we declared it was all right to be interned. We were the first *prisionniers volontaires* history has ever seen. After the Germans invaded the country, the French government had only to change the name of the firm; having been jailed because we were Germans, we were not freed because we were Jews. (Arendt 2007: 270)

Arendt graphically describes the troubled fate of Jewish refugees who were kicked about from one country to another, but she was concerned with a deeper issue. She wanted to understand the phenomenon of the masses of stateless human beings and refugees that had plagued Europe ever since the First World War. She concludes "We Refugees" with a more general claim about the political consequences of this new mass phenomenon. "Refugees driven from country to country represent the vanguard of their peoples – if they keep their identity. For the first time Jewish history is not separate but tied up with that of other nations. The comity of European peoples went to pieces when, and because, it allowed its weakest member to be excluded and persecuted" (Arendt 2007: 274).

"We Refugees," based on Arendt's personal experiences with her fellow refugees, raises fundamental questions about statelessness and refugees. She addresses these more forthrightly in a remarkable chapter in *The Origins,* "The Decline of the Nation-State and the End of the Rights of Man." Statelessness is "the newest mass phenomenon in contemporary history, and the existence of an ever-growing new people comprised of stateless persons [is] the most symptomatic group in contemporary politics" (Arendt 1976: 277).

Their existence can hardly be blamed on one factor alone, but if we consider the different groups among the stateless it appears that *every political event since the end of the first World War inevitably added a new category of those who lived outside the pale of law*, while none of the categories, no matter how the original constellation changed, could ever be renormalized. (Arendt 1976: 277, my emphasis)

When Arendt wrote this, she could scarcely have realized how relevant her observations would be in the second decade of the twenty-first century. Almost every significant political event during the past hundred years has resulted in the multiplication of new categories of refugees. Arendt focused primarily on European refugees, but this phenomenon is now global. There appears to be no end in sight to the increase in the numbers and categories of refugees. There is (with very few exceptions) increasing resistance to accepting refugees by sovereign nations. There are millions of persons in refugee camps with little hope that they will be able to return to their homes or find a new home. Arendt was one of the first major political thinkers to warn that the ever increasing categories and numbers of stateless persons and refugees would be the most symptomatic group of contemporary politics.

Arendt traces the beginning of the mass phenomenon of statelessness to the decline of the nation-state. The term "nation-state" is used today in a general manner to identify sovereign nations that govern bounded territories, but Arendt uses the expression in a much more precise manner. The modern nation-state arose in Europe at the end of the eighteenth century. She carefully distinguishes "nation" from "state." "Nation" refers to the dominant group with its culture, language, and shared history living in a bounded territory. "State" refers to the *legal* status of persons living in a territory – who are considered to be citizens with legal rights. From the time of the origins of the modern nation-state there was a tension between nation and state. Questions were raised about which persons were taken to be "true" members of a nation – which persons living in a territory were to be counted as citizens who deserved legal rights and which persons were to be excluded as non-citizens. This problem was exacerbated with the Minority Treaties established after the

First World War. These treaties were presumably instituted to protect minorities living in the newly created nation-states in Central and Eastern Europe. But these treaties stated in plain language what was becoming increasingly evident, "that only nationals could be citizens, only people of the same national origin could enjoy the full protection of legal institutions, that persons of different nationality needed some law of exception until or unless they were completely assimilated and divorced from their origin" (Arendt 1976: 275). Arendt exposes the hypocrisy and failure of the Minority Treaties. There was simply no effective international or state mechanism to protect the rights of minorities. The practical result of these treaties was to add new categories of stateless people – minorities fleeing from persecution in their "home" countries. In effect, nation and nationalism triumphed over state and the protection of legal rights. The danger of this development was inherent in the structure of the nation-state from the time of its beginning. Insofar as the establishment of nation-states coincided with the establishment of constitutional governments, they were based on the rule of law rather than arbitrary administration and despotism. "So that when the precarious balance between nation and state, between national interest and legal institutions broke down, the disintegration of this form of government and of organization of peoples came about with terrifying swiftness" (Arendt 1976: 275). Once again there is an uncanny parallel between the precarious balance of nation and state that Arendt describes and what is happening today with the rise of ugly forms of nationalism. Right-wing parties proclaim that only those who "truly" belong to a national culture deserve full legal rights. Only "true Frenchmen," "true Poles," "true Hungarians," and "true Americans" deserve full legal protection by the state.

There is a still further stage in the disintegration of the nation-state that became dominant in totalitarian countries but was also evident in non-totalitarian countries. This happened when people born in a nation-state were "denationalized." This was the fate of Jews in Germany long before the final solution of extermination. As soon as Hitler came to power, all sorts of laws were passed stripping Jews (and other "undesirable minorities") of juridical rights. Sovereign nations have always claimed an "absolute" right over matters of immigration, naturalization, and expulsion. Denationalization was not exclusively a systematic program of the Nazis; there was scarcely a country in Europe that did not pass some new legislation that allowed nations to get rid of or exclude "undesirable" inhabitants. Many people profess to be shocked by the policy of denaturalization carried out by the Nazis, but in our time many sovereign nations are instituting policies that have the same practical effect. Strictly speaking, from a narrow legal perspective, young children brought to the United States by undocumented parents, are not U.S. citizens. However, to end the program (i.e. DACA) whereby these children have been allowed to grow up, be educated, and work in America, and then deport them to countries in which they have never lived, has the same practical effect as denationalization.

When reading Arendt today on the tensions of nation and state, the ever new addition of masses of refugees, the plight of refugees who can't find a country to accept them, the mushrooming of refugee and internment camps, there is an eerie sense of contemporary relevance. The categories, causes, and regions where there are refugees today are certainly different. Yet it continues to be true that political events add ever new masses of stateless persons and refugees. Refugees are still the most symptomatic group in contemporary politics. Despite the growth of international organizations and NGOs concerned with refugees and human rights, sovereign nations still fiercely guard their "absolute" right to determine who they will and will not accept as refugees; all sorts of subterfuges are used to keep out refugees. Today, the very concept of sovereignty is being abused; it is used primarily to exclude "undesirable" refugees. The only "solution" to the current crisis has been the creation of ever more and larger refugee camps. There are now millions of persons – far more than when Arendt wrote *The Origins* – living in refugee camps with little hope that they will ever be able to leave them. This is the only "country" that the world has to offer those fleeing from the turmoil of war, persecution, and the misery of extreme poverty and famine. In short, virtually all the problems that Arendt highlights about statelessness and the refugee crisis continue to plague us – indeed, they have been intensified and exacerbated.

The Right to Have Rights

The status of being a stateless refugee raises difficult questions about the so-called Rights of Man, inalienable rights, and human rights. Arendt speaks about perplexities because she wants to identify the issues that we have to *think* about. She felt that most people do not really want to think – they prefer to ignore difficult political issues or use clichés to cover them up and dismiss them. She points to troublesome perplexities about the very idea of human rights. The French declaration of the Rights of Man and the American proclamation of "inalienable" rights, both pronounced at the end of the eighteenth century, were significant positive turning points in history. "It meant nothing more nor less than that from then on Man, and not God's command or the customs of history, should be the source of Law" (Arendt 1976: 290).

> Since the Rights of Man were proclaimed to be "inalienable," irreducible to and undeducible from other rights and laws, no authority was invoked for their establishment; Man himself was their source as well as their ultimate goal. No special law,

moreover, was deemed necessary to protect them because all laws were supposed to rest on them. Man appeared as the only sovereign in matters of law as the people was proclaimed the only sovereign in matters of government. (Arendt 1976: 291)

There was a paradox involved in the declarations of "inalienable rights" because these rights were ascribed to an abstract human being (Man) disconnected from actual historical concrete individuals. Neither the French nor the Americans intended these rights to apply to all human beings – not even to all human beings living within their territories. Despite these noble proclamations about the intrinsic dignity of every human being, it soon became evident that the question of human rights blended into the question of national emancipation. Only then could there be a government that could protect these inalienable rights for its citizens. "The Rights of Man, after all, had been defined as 'inalienable' because they were supposed to be independent of all governments; but it turned out that the moment human beings lacked their own government and had to fall back upon their minimum rights, no authority was left to protect them and no institution was willing to guarantee them" (Arendt 1976: 291–2). From the perspective of those who suffered the loss of their legal and civil rights, the loss of these rights meant the effective loss of inalienable rights. The Rights of Man, which are "presumably" universal and inalienable, proved – and continue to prove – unenforceable even in those countries whose constitutions are based upon them. Although this is disturbing in itself, there is a further problem. Despite attempts by international organizations such as the United Nations to specify what these human rights are, there are still sharp disagreements and confusion about what precisely are human inalienable rights. The international human rights movement has developed enormously since the mid-twentieth century. Now there are many international and national organizations concerned with widespread abuses that deprive people of their human rights. Nevertheless, at a deeper level, the problems that Arendt identifies regarding how to guarantee and protect inalienable rights continue to persist.

Arendt's passionate blend of integrating her own personal experience as a stateless German Jew with her thinking about the larger significance of stateless persons and refugees is poignantly illustrated in her trenchant description of the plight of the rightless. "The first loss which the rightless suffered was the loss of their homes, and this meant the loss of the entire social texture into which they were born and in which they established for themselves a distinct place in the world" (Arendt 1976: 293). Throughout history people have been uprooted from their homes. "What is unprecedented is not the loss of a home but the impossibility of finding a new one. Suddenly, there was no place on earth where migrants could go without the severest restrictions, no country where they would be assimilated, no territory where they could found a new community of their own" (Arendt 1976: 293). This was the experience of the majority of European Jews during the Nazi period. But today this experience is being repeated all over the world in the lives of people trying to escape from the wars, killing, and turmoil in their native countries. All sorts of devious measures are being adopted to block their entry.

The second loss of the rightless is the loss of any government protection. This too is not unprecedented. There has been a long tradition of granting asylum to individuals who have been persecuted and whose lives are endangered if forced to return to their native countries. The problem today is that even countries that still grant asylum have been overwhelmed by the sheer number of individuals seeking asylum. Asylum is a practice intended for exceptional individual cases, not for masses of refugees. What Arendt wrote about stateless refugees during the Nazi period is even more striking today. Being forced to leave one's country has little to do with what one has done or thought. The real calamity of the rightless is not just that they have lost their homes and government protection, but they no longer belong to any community whatsoever. Arendt describes the chilling "logic" of stripping people of their rights when she describes what happened in Nazi Germany.

> The calamity of the rightless is not that they are deprived of life, liberty, and the pursuit of happiness, or of equality before the law and freedom of opinion – formulas which were designed to solve problems *within* given communities – but that they no longer belong to any community whatsoever. Their plight is not that they are not equal before the law, but that no law exists for them, not

that they are oppressed but that nobody wants even to oppress them. Only in the last stage of a rather lengthy process is their right to live threatened; only if they remain "superfluous," if nobody can be found to "claim" them, may their lives be in danger. Even the Nazis started their extermination of the Jews by first depriving them of all legal status (the status of second-class citizenship) and cutting them off from the world of the living by herding them into ghettos and concentration camps; and before they set the gas chambers in motion they had carefully tested the ground and found out to their satisfaction that no country would claim these people. The point is that a condition of complete rightlessness was created before the right to live was challenged. (Arendt 1976: 295–6)

Arendt touches upon what is so frightening about the ever increasing masses of refugees living in refugee camps. Millions of people are now treated as if they are superfluous. Even though totalitarian regimes such as Nazi Germany and Stalin's Soviet Union no longer exist, we should acknowledge that there is a very thin line between depriving people of all rights and depriving them of life itself. The totalitarian "solution" to superfluousness still haunts us in a world where millions of people are treated as superfluous.

> The fundamental deprivation of human rights is manifested first and above all in the deprivation of a place in the world which makes opinions significant and actions effective. Something much more fundamental than freedom and justice, which are rights of all citizens, is at stake when belonging to the community into which one is born is no longer a matter of choice. . . . This extremity, and nothing else, is the situation of people deprived of human rights. They are deprived, not of the right of freedom, but of the right to action, not of the right to think whatever they please, but of the right to opinion. (Arendt 1976: 296)

In short, although the Rights of Man and the appeal to inalienable rights played an important role in the French and American Revolutions, Arendt is deeply suspicious of the appeal to abstract human rights – such that there are no effective institutions to guarantee and protect them. Arendt affirms that the most fundamental right is the "right to have rights," and this means the right to belong to some kind of organized community where rights are guaranteed and protected. "Not the loss of specific rights, then, but the loss of a community willing and able to guarantee any rights whatsoever, has been the calamity which has befallen ever-increasing numbers of people. Man, it turns out, can lose all so-called Rights of Man without losing his essential quality as man, his human dignity. *Only the loss of a polity itself expels him from humanity*" (Arendt 1976: 297, my emphasis).

In these passages about the right to have rights – the right to belong to a community that guarantees and protects its citizens, a community where individuals can express and share opinions and where one can act collectively with fellow human beings – we discern the origins of the major themes in her political thinking. She anticipates her investigation of plurality, action, speech, public space, empowerment, and public freedom – the web of concepts that constitutes the type of politics wherein one can express one's full humanity. She returns again and again to what it means to live in such a political community.

In *The Origins*, she returns to these themes in her analysis of the total domination that totalitarian regimes seek to achieve. By "dwelling on the horrors" of totalitarianism and by examining what totalitarian regimes sought to destroy in human beings, Arendt came to a deep appreciation of what is required for the expression of our humanity. When Arendt takes up the meaning of total domination, she begins her analysis by asserting that the concentration and extermination camps "serve as the laboratories in which the fundamental belief of totalitarianism that everything is possible is being verified" (Arendt 1976: 437). Totalitarian regimes aim to destroy the infinite plurality and differentiation of human beings. "The camps are meant not only to exterminate people and degrade human beings, but also to serve the ghastly experiment of eliminating, under scientifically controlled conditions, spontaneity itself as an expression of human behavior and of transforming the human personality into a mere thing" (Arendt 1976: 438). Arendt outlines a three-stage model of the "logic" of total domination. The first stage in the process of total domination is to kill the juridical person in man. This happens when people are stripped of their legal rights. This is the policy that the Nazis initiated long before the "Final Solution." The infamous Nuremberg laws systematically deprived the Jews and other "undesirables" of their rights. In the concentration camps, no one had any rights at all. Depriving people of their juridical rights is just the beginning of the logic of total domination.

The second stage in preparing living corpses is the murder of the moral person. This occurs when even martyrdom becomes impossible. Totalitarian terror achieved its most terrible triumph when even decisions of conscience became impossible.

> When a man is faced with the alternative of betraying and thus murdering his friends or sending his wife and children, for whom he is in every sense responsible, to their death; when even suicide would mean the immediate murder of his own family – how is he to decide? The alternative is no longer between good and evil, but between murder and murder. Who could solve the moral dilemma of the Greek mother, who was allowed by the Nazis to choose which of her three children should be killed? (Arendt 1976: 452)

But this is not yet the worst. There is still a third stage in this "logic" of total domination.

After the killing of the juridical person and the murder of the moral person, the one thing that still prevents human beings from becoming living corpses is their spontaneity and individual differentiation. "After murder of the moral person and annihilation of the juridical person, the destruction of individuality is almost always successful. . . . For to destroy individuality is to destroy spontaneity, man's power to begin something new out of his own resources, something that cannot be explained on the basis of reactions to environment and events" (Arendt 1976: 455). The ultimate aim of totalitarianism is to make human beings as human beings super-fluous. "What totalitarian ideologies therefore aim at is not the transformation of the outside world or the revolutionizing transmutation of society, but the transformation of human nature itself" (Arendt 1976: 458). Arendt's focus on eliminating human spontaneity, individuality, and plurality – systematically transforming human beings into "living corpses" – calls to mind the figure of the *Musselmann* in the death camps. Primo Levi gives a vivid description of this phenomenon, which he experienced in Auschwitz.

Their life is short, but their number endless, they are the *Musselmänner*, the drowned, form the backbone of the camp, an anonymous mass, continually renewed and always identical of non-men who march and labor in silence, the divine spark dead within them, already too empty to really suffer. One hesitates to call them living; one hesitates to call their death death, in the face of which they have no fear as they are too tired to understand.

They crowd my memory with their faceless presence and if I could enclose all the evil of our time in one image, I would choose this image which is familiar to me; an emaciated man, with head drooped and shoulders curved, on whose face and in whose eyes not a trace of thought is to be seen. (Levi 1996: 56)

Although she did not use the expression "*Musselmann*," Arendt thought that these "living corpses" epitomized an unprecedented form of absolute or radical evil. We have nothing to fall back on to understand this phenomenon that confronts us with its overpowering reality and breaks down all standards we know. "There is only one thing that seems discernable: we may say that radical evil has emerged in connection with a system in which all men have become equally superfluous" (Arendt 1976: 459). Arendt's analysis of the "logic" of total domination is closely related to her worry about the consequences of the creation of ever new categories of superfluous stateless refugees. She concludes her discussion of total domination with a warning – a warning that we should take with the utmost seriousness today.

> The danger of the corpse factories and the holes of oblivion is that today, with populations and homelessness everywhere on the increase, masses of people are continuously rendered superfluous if we continue to think of our world in utilitarian terms. Political, social, and economic events everywhere are in silent conspiracy with totalitarian instruments devised to make men superfluous. ... The Nazis and the Bolsheviks can be sure that their factories of annihilation which demonstrate the swiftest solution to the problem of over-population, of economically superfluous and socially rootless human masses, are as much of an attraction as a warning. (Arendt 1976: 459)

The most disturbing sentence in *The Origins* is the last sentence in the section. "Total Domination":

"Totalitarian solutions may well survive the fall of totalitarian regimes in the form of strong temptations which will come up wherever it seems impossible to alleviate political, social and economic misery in a manner worthy of man" (Arendt 1976: 459). Arendt, who always insisted that thinking required making clear distinctions, argues that totalitarianism was an unprecedented movement and regime – not to be confused with authoritarian governments, dictatorship, or tyranny. No other regime in history ever engaged in a comparable project of systematic total domination with the aim of destroying any human vestige of individuality, spontaneity, and plurality. No other regime had sought to transform human beings into something that is not human. Throughout history there have been massacres and genocides; but what she took to be distinctive about totalitarianism is the systematic attempt to transform human nature itself – to show that everything is possible. Totalitarianism as a form of government may have ended with the defeat of the Nazis and the collapse of the Soviet Union, but totalitarian "solutions" have been – and continue to be – strong temptations. We witness this in the genocides and the use (as well as the justification) of torture since the fall of totalitarian regimes. With the ever increasing addition of masses of stateless people and refugees throughout the world who are treated as if they are superfluous, we should take seriously Arendt's warning that there is a fragile line between destroying the right to have rights and destroying life itself.

Loyal Opposition: Arendt's Critique of Zionism

When Arendt fled from Germany in 1933, her greatest disappointment stemmed from the way in which many of her friends and acquaintances tolerated or cooperated with the Nazis. *Gleichschalltung* (co-ordination) was the rule among intellectuals. She found this repulsive, and she made the decision when she left Germany to become active in opposing the Nazis. She asked herself what she could do as a Jew. "[B]elonging to Judaism had become my own problem, and my own problem was political. Purely political! I wanted to go into practical work, exclusively and only Jewish work. With this in mind I then looked for work in France"

(Arendt 1994: 12). Arendt never joined any Zionist party, and she never considered Aliyah ("going up," or return) to Palestine. When she was living in Paris she did, however, work for Youth Aliyah, the organization that sent endangered European Jewish youths to Palestine. She even accompanied a group of Youth Aliyah trainees to Palestine in 1935. Arendt's motivation for working with Zionists was that they, unlike Jewish parvenus and assimilationists, were active politically in opposing Hitler and the Nazis. Arendt's attraction to Zionism in the 1930s was shaped more by Bernard Lazare than by more prominent Zionists such as Theodor Herzl or Chaim Weizmann. Lazare was involved in the reporting of the Dreyfus affair and defending Dreyfus against fabricated lies. Lazare belonged to what Arendt called "the hidden tradition of the Jewish pariah" – a tradition that incudes Heinrich Heine, Charlie Chaplin (who actually was not a Jew but epitomized the comic Jewish pariah mentality), Bernard Lazare, and Franz Kafka. What distinguished Lazare is that he was a "conscious pariah," a rebel who believed that the Jewish people should join with other oppressed groups to fight injustice.

Living in the France of the Dreyfus affair, Lazare could appreciate at first hand the pariah quality of Jewish existence. But he knew where the solution lay: in contrast to his unemancipated brethren who accept their pariah status automatically and unconsciously, the emancipated Jew must awake to an awareness of his position and, conscious of it, become a rebel against it – the champion of an oppressed people. His fight for freedom is part and parcel of that which all the downtrodden of Europe must wage to achieve national and social liberation. (Arendt 2007: 283)

Arendt herself was a "conscious pariah" in the tradition of Lazare. She too believed that one should join with others to fight for justice and freedom. This is the primary reason for her original decision to work with the Zionists. But the situation changed in the 1940s. As the gruesome details of the mass murder of the Jews by the Nazis were being revealed, there was a growing international sympathy for the plight of the European Jews. At the same time the British, who had been assigned the Mandate over Palestine by the League of Nations, were confronting turmoil, terrorism, and riots by both Jews and Arabs. They were eager to give up the Mandate and get out of Palestine. Zionists saw this as an opportunity to create a Jewish state.

What alarmed Arendt about the proclamations of the Zionists is that they increasingly ignored the Arab question – the fact that the majority of people living in Palestine were Arabs, not Jews. Arendt never hesitated to express her opinions in the strongest possible language. She vociferously objected to the program that the Zionists adopted in 1942 whereby it was proposed that the Jews in Palestine would grant minority rights to the majority population (Arabs). She argued that for fifty years, from the time of the first Zionist Aliyah to Palestine, Zionists ignored, obscured, and suppressed the explosive issue of Jewish–Arab relations in Palestine. Arendt's sharpest critique of Zionism was provoked by a resolution adopted unanimously at the October 1944 meeting of the American Zionists (and later affirmed by the World Zionist Organization). The resolution called for the establishment of a "free and democratic Jewish commonwealth. ... [which] shall embrace the whole of Palestine, undivided and undiminished" (Arendt 2007: 343). For Arendt this was the last straw. It was a decisive turning point in Zionist history, at which moderate Zionists completely capitulated to more extremist revisionists.

The article she wrote, "Zionism Reconsidered," damning the resolution was more vehement than anything she had previously written on Jewish or Zionist issues. She employed all her rhetorical skills – irony, sarcasm, scorn, and blunt denunciation. Her passion was provoked by her anger and disappointment with the most extreme Zionist ideologists. The language of "Zionism Reconsidered" was so inflammatory that the Jewish intellectual journal *Commentary* refused to publish it. It was eventually published in the *Menorah Journal.* Arendt knew that her voice was a minority one and that her controversial opinion was being shouted down by others, but this did not deter her. She wanted an honest, forthright discussion of Arab–Jewish issues at a time when most Zionists refused to face reality. One of her favorite quotations, which she cited frequently, became a motto, *victrix causa diis placuit, sed victa Catoni* ("the victorious cause pleases the gods, but the defeated one pleases Cato"). This phrase took on a special meaning for Arendt. Not only did the victorious cause please the gods, but historians – especially modern historians – were overwhelmingly biased toward giving weight to the "victorious" causes and movements in history. Hannah Arendt, like Walter Benjamin, who had deeply influenced her thinking, was critical of this bias – where history is taken to be a narrative of "progressive" victories.

Arendt knew from direct experience what it was like to express a dissenting opinion – to be among the "loyal opposition" – only to be silenced or condemned for betrayal. Like Bernard Lazare – long before the Eichmann controversy – Arendt was becoming a pariah among her own people. She was disturbed not only by the Zionists' turn to extreme revisionism but also by the growing pressures toward ideological conformity. In her quest for the meaning and dignity of politics, she highlights the importance of public debate of conflicting opinions. The tendency toward ideological unanimity – the displacing of different perspectives on a common world with a single "truth" of one ideology – is the most ominous tendency in the contemporary world. This is the tendency that was "perfected" by totalitarian movements through their use of terror. In her article "To Save a Jewish Homeland," written after hostilities broke out between Jews and Arabs, she wrote:

> Unanimity of opinion is a very ominous phenomenon, and one characteristic of our modern mass age. It destroys social and personal life, which is based on the fact that we are different by nature and by conviction. To hold different opinions and to be aware that other people think differently on the same issue shields us from Godlike certainty which stops all discussion and reduces social relationships to those of an ant heap. A unanimous public opinion tends to eliminate bodily those who differ, for mass unanimity is not the result of agreement, but an expression of fanaticism and hysteria. In contrast to agreement, unanimity does not stop at certain well-defined objects, but spreads like an infection into every related issue. (Arendt 2007: 391–2)

When I turn to the explicit discussion of Arendt's positive conception of politics and public freedom, we will see how central this conflict and debate about a plurality of opinions is for her positive understanding of politics. But here I emphasize how her thinking about politics was grounded in her experience of dissenting from Zionist ideological unanimity.

Arendt argued for creating a Jewish *homeland* in Palestine, *not* a Jewish nation-state. A Jewish homeland would be a place where Jewish culture could grow and thrive, a place where Jews would learn to live with Arabs in a joint community, where all citizens would have equal rights. For most Zionists at the time this was not only an absurd utopian proposal; it was an act of betrayal. They saw no alternative to the Zionists' dream of founding a Jewish nation-state. Arendt anticipated that the creation of such a Jewish state would foster militant nationalism among both Jews and Arabs.

On November 29, 1947, the General Assembly of the newly created United Nations voted in favor of the partition of Palestine. The problem that plagued the old League of Nations was also to plague the United Nations. There was no clear indication about how such a partition would be instituted and enforced. Soon after the vote, war broke out between Palestinian Jews and their multiple Arab enemies. Arendt was fully aware of the long history of riots and violence between Arabs and Jews in Palestine, but nevertheless in 1948, when the fighting was still raging, she wrote: "The idea of Arab–Jewish cooperation, though never realized on any scale and today seemingly farther off than ever, is not an idealistic daydream but a sober statement of the fact that without it the whole Jewish venture in Palestine is doomed" (Arendt 2007: 396). Arendt expressed her sympathy for Judah Magnes, the president of the Hebrew University who led a small party, *Ihud* (Unity), consisting primarily of intellectuals (including Martin Buber). Arendt shared their vision of a unified country of Jews and Arabs living together. Even when the war between Jews and Arabs erupted and the outcome was still unclear, Arendt made a chilling prediction of what might happen even if the Jews were to win the war.

And even if the Jews were to win the war, its end would find the unique possibilities and the unique achievements of Zionism in Palestine destroyed. The land that would come into being would be something quite other than the dream of world Jewry, Zionist and non-Zionist. The "victorious" Jews would live surrounded by an entirely hostile Arab population, secluded inside ever-threatened borders, absorbed with physical self-defense to a degree that would submerge all other interests and activities. The growth of a Jewish culture would cease to be the concern of the whole people; social experiments would have to be discarded as impractical luxuries; political thought would center around military strategy; economic development would be determined exclusively by the needs of war. And all this would be the fate of a nation that – no matter how many immigrants it could still absorb and how far it extended its boundaries (the whole of Palestine and Transjordan is the insane Revisionist demand) – would still remain a very small people greatly outnumbered by hostile neighbors. (Arendt 2007: 396–7)

Given her pessimistic portrayal of what might happen, what did she propose could still be done? She recommended that the United Nations "summon up the courage in this unprecedented situation to take an unprecedented step by going to those Jewish and Arab individuals who at present are isolated because of their records as sincere believers in Arab–Jewish cooperation, and asking them to negotiate a truce" (Arendt 2007: 399). Arendt was not recommending a division of Palestine into two nation-states. She consistently argued that the nation-state (with its inherent tensions between nation and state) was not a viable solution.

So what was the alternative that she proposed? This was no longer a theoretical question but one that had practical urgency. We discover here one of the first sketches of Arendt's alternative to the nation-state – what she later called the council system. With explicit reference to the proposals of Judah Magnes and *Ihud*, Arendt wrote:

> The alternative proposition of a federated state, also recently endorsed by Dr. Magnes, is much more realistic: despite the fact that it establishes a common government of two different peoples, it avoids the troublesome majority–minority constellation, which is insoluble by definition. A federated structure moreover would have to rest on Jewish–Arab community councils, which would mean that the Jewish–Arab conflict would be resolved on the lowest and most promising level of proximity and neighborliness. (Arendt 2007: 400)

In the hysterical atmosphere that prevailed at the time, Arendt knew that her proposal for a federated state based on local Arab–Jewish councils would be attacked by Zionists as a "stab in the back." But she forcefully argued that this was the only "realistic" way to save the idea of a Jewish homeland. Against the overwhelming unanimity of opinion and enthusiasm by Jewish communities all over the world for founding a Jewish nation-state, Arendt thought of herself as a member of the "loyal opposition." She concluded "To Save the Jewish Homeland" by outlining a set of concrete conditions for a realistic solution to the Arab–Jewish problem in Palestine. Her final proposal summed up her idea of a federated state based on local councils. "Local self-government and mixed Jewish–Arab municipal and rural councils on a small scale and as numerous as possible, are the only *realistic* political measures that can eventually lead to the political emancipation of Palestine. It is still not too late" (Arendt 2007: 401, my emphasis).

Unfortunately, it *was* too late. There was no significant group willing to take Arendt seriously. No one was willing to listen to Arendt when she declared that there would never be peace in the region unless Jews and Arabs directly negotiate and find ways to cooperate. Like Cato, she realized that she was defending a defeated cause. Despite all the changes that have taken place in the Middle East since the time she wrote about these issues in the 1940s, her observations and warnings have a remarkable relevance today. She was extraordinarily perceptive about the deep problems and unresolved issues that continue to persist. She was insightful about the ominous dangers of the unanimity of opinion that seeks to marginalize and silence all dissent. She warned about how Israel as a Jewish nation-state would continue to be plagued with the problem of the rights and citizenship of its Arab population – a problem exacerbated by the occupation of the West Bank since 1967. Considering the history of failures to resolve the Israeli–Palestinian conflict over the past seventy years, no one can predict what will happen in the future – especially in light of the more general turmoil in the region. But one thing should be absolutely clear. There will never be anything resembling peace in the Middle East unless there is an attempt to confront honestly the problems that Arendt so brilliantly identified.

Racism and Segregation

Throughout her life Arendt was involved in heated controversies. For better or worse, she expressed her opinions in the strongest possible language, touched raw nerves, and provoked sharp criticism. She was often insightful, but at times she could also be obtuse and guilty of what she took to be the worst sin of intellectuals – imposing her own categories on the world instead of being sensitive to the complexities of reality. In the 1950s, soon after the appearance of *The Human Condition*, when Arendt was becoming better known as a public intellectual, she provoked a fierce controversy when she published "Reflections on Little Rock." In 1954 the United States Supreme Court, in the landmark decision, *Brown v. Board of Education of Topeka*, unanimously ruled that segregation of the public schools violated the Fourteenth Amendment of the Constitution. The decision and the implementation of integration were strongly resisted throughout the Southern states. On September 4, 1957, Elizabeth Eckford, a fifteen-year-old black girl, who now had the legal right to attend Central High School in Little Rock, set off for the first day of school. The Governor of Arkansas had sent the Arkansas National Guard with bayonets to turn her and others away from entering the school. A photograph of a dignified

Elizabeth threatened by a screaming white mob appeared in newspapers throughout the world. It was shocking and became an iconic image of the depth of hatred and ugly discrimination against Blacks in America. Soon after this incident, the editors of *Commentary* commissioned Arendt to write about Little Rock. The article she submitted was judged so inflammatory and offensive that the editors hesitated to publish it without a reply from Sidney Hook. Arendt withdrew the article, but when resistance to school integration continued, she agreed to publish it with a prefatory note in *Dissent* in 1959.

Arendt strongly opposed federally imposed integration of public schools. Using categories that she had elaborated in *The Human Condition*, she drew a sharp distinction between the political, the social, and the private. She claimed that social discrimination should not be outlawed by political means. If white parents want to send their children to schools where there are only white children, the government has no right to interfere. "The government can legitimately take no steps against social discrimination because government can act only in the name of equality – a principle which does not obtain in the social sphere" (Arendt 1959: 53). Furthermore, "the government has no right to interfere with the prejudices and discriminatory practices of society; it has not only the right but the duty to make sure that these practices are not legally enforced" (Arendt 1959: 53). She even suggested that Negro (black) parents were using their children to fight adult political battles. She thought that education should be a private matter and (except for insuring compulsory public education) the government should not interfere with parental decisions about how to educate their children. And, finally, she defended the idea of states' rights based on her conception of the balance of power between the federal and state governments. At the time, many Southern politicians argued that the federal government had *no* right to interfere with the right of states to *enforce* segregation in the public schools. Thus, Arendt failed to understand the disastrous consequences of hostile political, economic, and social discrimination of Blacks in America. She failed to understand how the appeal to "state's rights" had been abused to enforce all sorts of ugly discriminatory practices against Blacks.

Once Arendt formed an opinion, she rarely backed down, but in this instance she admitted her misjudgment when Ralph Ellison, the famous black writer, accused her of failing to understand the experience of "people who must live in a society without recognition, real status, but who are involved in the ideals of that society and who are trying to make their way, trying to determine their true position and their rightful position within it." He charged Arendt with failing to understand the ideal of sacrifice among Southern Blacks. "Hannah Arendt's failure to grasp the importance of this ideal among Southern Negroes caused her to fly off into left field in her 'Reflections on Little Rock' in which she charged Negro parents with exploiting their children during the struggle to integrate the schools. But she has absolutely no conception of what goes on in the minds of Negro parents when they send their kids through those lines of hostile people" (Ellison's comments are cited in Young-Bruehl 1982: 316). When Arendt read Ellison's remarks, she was not defensive. She wrote him a letter in which she acknowledged her error. "It is precisely this ideal of sacrifice which I didn't understand"; she failed to grasp "the element of stark violence, of elementary, bodily fear in the situation" (Young-Bruehl 1982: 316).

Despite Arendt's acknowledgment of her misjudgment in a private communication to Ellison, sharp criticism of "Reflections on Little Rock" persists right up to the present. Danielle S. Allen and Kathryn T. Gines have written detailed critiques, pointing out Arendt's factual errors and misguided opinions (Allen 2004 and Gines 2014). I agree with most of the substantive points of these critics. I do not think that Arendt understood the depth and political consequences (even according to her *own* concept of politics) of vicious discrimination against Blacks in America. But I do not think that Arendt was "a white supremacist" or an "anti-Black racist" – epithets that have frequently been used to characterize her views (although not by Allen and Gines). I also want to suggest that if we think with Arendt against Arendt, then we discover resources in her writings for confronting the perniciousness of racism today.

It is important to understand her thinking about racism in her earlier writings, especially in *The Origins*. One of the primary issues that Arendt confronts in *The Origins* is the biological racism of the Nazis that led to the Final Solution of extermination. In her search for the subterranean elements that crystallized into totalitarianism, she focuses on the racism that was intrinsic to imperialism. Arendt distinguishes between colonialism and imperialism. She writes that "through centuries the extermination of native peoples went hand in hand with colonization in America, Australia and Africa." But something different and much more vicious occurred when the ideology of expansion for expansion's sake became the dominant ideology of imperialism (Arendt 1976: 440). Arendt presents a brutal and graphic description of the massacres and genocides that took place in the "scramble for Africa." No longer was there even a pretense of colonial regulation of subjected African populations. Imperialist racism "justified" the brutal administrative massacre of millions of native Africans as a legitimate way of conducting foreign policy. This imperialist, murderous, ideological racism anticipated the racist ideology of the Nazis. Throughout her life Arendt condemned racist ideology. Even in *On Violence*, where once again she makes injudicious and offensive remarks about American Negroes, she asserts:

Racism, as distinguished from race, is not a fact of life, but an ideology, and the deeds it leads to are not reflex actions, but deliberate acts based on pseudo-scientific theories. Violence in interracial struggle is always murderous, but it is not 'irrational'; it is the logical and rational consequence of racism, by which I do not mean some rather vague prejudices on either side, but an explicit ideological system. (Arendt 1970: 76)

Despite Arendt's insights into the violent character of racism as an ideological system in a European context, she failed to appreciate its relevance to the experience of Blacks in America. She did not object to discrimination in the social realm; she objected only to its legal enforcement. She characterizes segregation as a social phenomenon that needs to be sharply distinguished from what is truly political. "[I]t is not the social custom of segregation that is unconstitutional, but its *legal enforcement*" (Arendt: 1959: 49). Arendt, who is famous for drawing distinctions, characterizes discrimination in a somewhat Pollyanna-ish manner. She *blurs* the distinction between benign discrimination and the vicious, exclusionary, humiliating discrimination experienced by many Blacks. "If as a Jew I wish to spend my vacation only in the company of Jews, I cannot see how anyone can reasonably prevent my doing so, just as I see no reason why other resorts should not cater to a clientele that wishes not to see Jews while on a holiday" (Arendt 1959: 52).

But it is grossly insensitive to compare this type of social discrimination (which is not so benign) where I *freely* choose with whom I want to spend my vacation with the violent discrimination that Blacks *coercively* experienced in their everyday lives. Arendt misleadingly *imposes* her distinctions between the political, social, and private. "Society is that curious, somewhat hybrid realm between the political and the private in which, since the beginning of the modern age, most men have spent the greater part of their lives" (Arendt 1959: 51). (For a critical discussion of Arendt's distinctions between the political, the social, and the private, see Bernstein 1986.)

What is perplexing about Arendt's obtuseness is that there are many resources in her writings for developing a more sympathetic and nuanced understanding of racial discrimination. One must be careful about drawing analogies between Jews and Blacks, but Arendt might have drawn upon her own experience when she declared that when one is attacked as a Jew one must defend oneself

as a Jew, not as a German, not as an upholder of
the Rights of Man. Why isn't this just as relevant
to Blacks when they are clearly attacked as Blacks?
Or again, Arendt might have seen the relevance
of her understanding of the Jewish pariah who is
treated as an outcast and should become a "conscious rebel" like Bernard Lazare – who believed
that one must resist and join with others in fighting oppression. In Arendt's discussion of Franz
Kafka as a Jewish pariah, she beautifully describes
the profound dilemma of social outcasts, who
want nothing more than to be treated as human
beings and as normal members of human society:
"to become people like other people." What she
says about "K," the hero of Kafka's novel, *The
Castle*, might well be said about Blacks and other
minority groups that suffer from humiliating discrimination. "It was not his fault that this society
had ceased to be human, and that, trapped within
its meshes, those of its members who were really
men of goodwill were forced to function within it
as something exceptional and abnormal – saints
or madmen" (Arendt 2007: 293). Indeed, Arendt
might well have developed her insight that the
problem is not simply one of what Blacks should
or should not do, but a problem of the larger

white society in which they live. "If a Negro in a white community is considered as a Negro and nothing else, he loses along with the right to equality that freedom of action which is specifically human, all his deeds are now explained as 'necessary' consequences of some 'Negro' qualities; he has become some specimen of an animal species, called man" (Arendt 1976: 301–2).

I have been critical of Arendt's reasoning in "Reflections on Little Rock," but looking back from the present, one should also see how prescient she was. There were great hopes in the 1950s that integration of the schools would be a major step in solving the "Negro question" in America. Arendt was deeply skeptical about this. Many have argued that the *de facto* segregation of schools today is as bad or worse than it was in 1957. She was skeptical that even Civil Rights laws would end discrimination, and she thought that the United States had never honestly faced the "original crime" of excluding Blacks and natives from "the original *consensus universalis* of the American republic. There was nothing in the Constitution or in the intent that could be so construed as to include the slave people in the original compact" (Arendt 1972: 90). She was ridiculed at the time for claiming that the miscegenation laws that existed in twenty-nine states – laws that prohibited marriage and sexual relations between Whites and Blacks – were a far more flagrant breach of the Constitution than segregation of the schools. It was only in 1967 that the Supreme Court declared that these laws were unconstitutional. Arendt was also ahead of her times when she emphatically declared that "the right to marry whoever one wishes is an elementary human right" (Arendt 1959: 49). Without exonerating Arendt's misjudgments about Little Rock, I believe we find resources in her writings for thinking about and resisting racism, which is still so prevalent in the world today.

The Banality of Evil

When *Eichmann in Jerusalem* was initially published in 1963 as a five-part article in *The New Yorker*, Hannah Arendt was viciously attacked. She was accused of exonerating Eichmann, making him appear more attractive than his Jewish victims and blaming the Jews for bringing about their own extermination. Many were offended by Arendt's "ironic" style. Some accused her of being "flippant" and "malicious." The phrase the "banality of evil" seemed to trivialize the extermination of millions of Jews. The attack became personal. Arendt was accused of being a self-hating Jew. There were even attempts to suppress the publication of her book. Several of her oldest and closest friends broke off relations with her. Reading *Eichmann in Jerusalem* today, more than fifty years after its publication, it is difficult to understand the intensity of the furor it created. There are serious criticisms that can be (and have been) raised about many of her key claims. Her brief discussion of the role of the Jewish councils justifiably aroused a great deal of outrage. The Jewish councils consisted of prominent Jews selected by the Nazis to organize Jewish communities and ghettos. When the extermination process began, the Jewish councils were assigned the task of filling the Nazi quotas. Arendt is harsh in her judgment of the Jewish leadership.

Wherever Jews lived, there were recognized Jewish leaders, and this leadership, almost without exception, cooperated in one way or another, for one reason or another, with the Nazis. The whole truth was that if the Jewish people had really been unorganized and leaderless, there would have been chaos and plenty of misery but the total number victims would hardly have been between four and a half and six million people. (Arendt 1965a: 125)

This is one of the most inflammatory and irresponsible claims made in Arendt's report. She fails to take account of the wide range of behavior of these Jewish leaders, some of whom committed suicide rather than follow Nazi orders. The truth is that no one can say for certain how many Jews would have been murdered even if Jewish councils had never existed.

Even in light of legitimate criticisms of her report, there is, nevertheless, an enormous disparity between what Arendt wrote and the "image" of her book that her critics condemned. The charge that Arendt exonerated Eichmann is completely false. She considered him to be one of the "greatest criminals" of the time. Unlike many who challenged the legitimacy of the trial, she strongly defended the right of the Israeli court to try Eichmann. Throughout her report she argued that Eichmann was fully responsible for the crimes that he committed. Although she was critical, even scornful, of the melodramatic performance of the chief prosecutor, she expressed her highest admiration for the three judges who tried Eichmann. She completely endorsed their judgment concerning Eichmann's responsibility and guilt. "What the judgment had to say on this point was more than correct, it was the truth" (Arendt 1965a: 246). When the court finally sentenced Eichmann to death, Arendt endorsed the death sentence. When she used the phrase "the banality of evil," she was not advancing a *theory* about Nazi evil but describing what she took to be a factual matter. Eichmann's deeds were monstrous, but Eichmann was not a monster. He was banal and ordinary, caught up in his own clichés and language rules. In the postscript to *Eichmann in Jerusalem* she explained what she meant by "the banality of evil."

[W]hen I speak of the banality of evil, I do so only on the strictly factual level, pointing to a phenomenon which stared one in the face at the trial. Eichmann was not Iago and not Macbeth and nothing would have been farther from his mind than to determine with Richard III "to prove a villain." Except for an extraordinary diligence in looking out for his personal advancement he had no motives at all. . . . He *merely*, to put the matter colloquially, *never realized what he was doing*. It was precisely this lack of imagination which enabled him to sit for months on end facing a German Jew who was conducting the police interrogation, pouring out his heart to the man and explaining again and again how it was that he reached only the rank of lieutenant colonel in the S.S. and that it had not been his fault that he was not promoted. . . . He was not stupid. It was sheer thoughtlessness – something by no means identical with stupidity – that predisposed him to become one of the greatest criminals of that period. (Arendt 1965a: 287–8, italics original)

When Arendt says that he "never realized what he was doing" she doesn't mean that he acted blindly. He was masterful in arranging the transportation of Jews to concentration and extermination camps. But he lacked the imagination to see things from the perspective of his victims. He lacked what Kant had described as an "enlarged mentality." In a lecture that Arendt gave at The New School for Social Research in 1970, she returned to the banality of evil, expanding on the point she made in *Eichmann in Jerusalem.*

Some years ago, reporting the trial of Eichmann in Jerusalem, I spoke of "the banality of evil" and meant with this no theory or doctrine but something quite factual, the phenomenon of evil deeds committed on a gigantic scale, which could not be traced to any particularity of wickedness, pathology, or ideological conviction in the doer, whose only personal distinction was perhaps extraordinary shallowness. However monstrous the deeds were, the doer was neither monstrous nor demonic, and the only specific characteristic one could detect in his past as well as in his behavior during the trial and the preceding police examination was something entirely negative: it was not stupidity but a curious, quite authentic inability to think. He functioned in the role of prominent war criminal as well as he had under the Nazi regime; he had not the slightest difficulty in accepting an entirely different set of rules. He knew that what he had once considered his duty was now called a crime, and he accepted this new code of judgment as though it were nothing but another language rule. (Arendt 1971: 417)

Ever since the publication of *Eichmann in Jerusalem* there has been an extensive debate

about the accuracy of Arendt's depiction of
Eichmann. My own view is that it is not accurate.
We now know much more about Eichmann's
past in Germany as well as his life in Argentina,
where he lived when he escaped from Germany.
In Argentina he was closely associated with other
former Nazis and boasted about (even exagger-
ated) his role in the Final Solution. I agree with
the judgment of the distinguished historian of
the Holocaust, Christopher Browning, when
he writes: "I consider Arendt's concept of 'the
banality of evil' a very important insight for
understanding many of the perpetrators of the
Holocaust, but not Eichmann himself. Arendt
was fooled by Eichmann's strategy of self-
representation in part because there were so many
perpetrators of the kind he was pretending to be"
(Browning 2003: 3–4).

One might think that if Arendt was mistaken
in her historical "factual" judgment of Eichmann
– that although he appeared banal and cliché-
ridden in the Jerusalem court, he was actually
more fanatical and ideologically motivated as a
Nazi – then this puts an end to the matter. I do
not think so. On the contrary, there is something extremely important about the idea of the

banality of evil, and when properly understood, it has significant relevance for us today. One of the reasons why her phrase provoked such a strong reaction is that she was calling into question a deeply entrenched way of thinking about evil – one that is psychologically appealing and frequently becomes dominant in times of perceived crisis. We tend to think of good and evil in absolute terms – as a stark dichotomy. There are heroes and villains. There are vicious perpetrators and innocent victims. If one commits "monstrous deeds" as Eichmann did, then one *must* be a monster or demonic. He *must* have sadistic, monstrous, antisemitic intentions and motives – or be pathological. He *must* be like the great villains portrayed in literature, or even like the villains portrayed in popular films and culture. There is something so deep and entrenched about this way of thinking that to call it into question is extremely disturbing. Eichmann was certainly portrayed as demonic by Gideon Hausner, the chief prosecutor. Eichmann was the embodiment of antisemitism dating back to Pharaoh in Egypt and the mastermind of the Final Solution (which is clearly false). Arendt also firmly rejected the "cog theory" – the idea that Eichmann was merely a cog in a vast bureaucratic machine. In response to the claim that someone was merely a cog or a wheel in a system, it is always appropriate to ask in matters of law and morality, "And why did you become a cog and continue to function in this way?"

Arendt's major point is that we should not mythologize evil. Many years before the trial, in an exchange of letters with her mentor and friend Karl Jaspers, he wrote to her that he objected to speaking about a guilt that goes beyond all criminal guilt because it takes on a streak of satanic greatness. It is inappropriate to speak of the demonic element in Hitler and other Nazis. In 1946 he wrote: "It seems to me that we have to see these things in their total banality, in their prosaic triviality, because that's what truly characterizes them. Bacteria can cause epidemics that wipe out nations, but they remain merely bacteria" (Arendt and Jaspers 1992: 62). Seventeen years later when Gershom Scholem criticized the idea of the banality of evil, Arendt answered him in a way that echoes Jaspers's earlier remark. "It is indeed my opinion now that evil is never 'radical,' that it is only extreme, and that it possesses neither depth nor any demonic dimension. It can overgrow and lay to waste the whole world precisely because it spreads like a fungus on the surface. It is 'thought-defying,' as I said, because thought tries to reach some depth, to go to the roots, and the moment it concerns itself with evil, it is frustrated because there is nothing. That is its 'banality'" (Arendt 2007: 471). (For a further discussion of the meaning of the banality of evil and how it is related to Arendt's characterization of radical evil in *The Origins,* see Bernstein 1996 and Bernstein 2016.) The idea of the banality of evil is still relevant today because we need to face up to the fact that one doesn't have to be a monster to commit horrendous evil deeds. To claim that people can commit evil deeds for banal reasons is to confront the reality in which we live today: "The sad truth of the matter is that most evil is done by people who never made up their mind to be either good or bad" (Arendt 1971: 438).

Truth, Politics, and Lying

When the furor over the publication of *Eichmann in Jerusalem* intensified, Arendt's good friend Mary McCarthy urged Arendt to answer her critics. Arendt initially resisted, but later she told Mary that she intended to write an essay "Truth and Politics" in order to deal with issues raised by the attacks. Arendt believed that most of the criticism of *Eichmann in Jerusalem* was directed against an "image" created by her critics, not what she actually wrote. She felt that all sorts of lies were circulating about her report of the Eichmann trial. She wanted to raise basic questions about lying, truth, and politics. Arendt begins her essay in a most arresting manner.

> No one has ever doubted that truth and politics are on rather bad terms with each other, and no one, as far as I know, has ever counted truthfulness among the political virtues. Lies have always been regarded as necessary and justifiable tools not only of the politician's or the demagogue's but also of the statesman's trade. Why is this so? And what does it mean for the nature and dignity of the political realm, on the one side, and for the nature and dignity of truth and truthfulness, on the other? Is it the essence of truth to be impotent and of the essence of power to be deceitful? (Arendt 1977: 227–8)

The history of the conflict of truth and politics is an old and complicated one. Arendt divides her discussion into two parts: the first concerns the question of "rational truth"; the second – more relevant to contemporary discussions – concerns "factual truth." By "rational truth" Arendt means such truths as mathematical truths like 2 + 2 = 4 or, more significantly, the type of truths that Plato claims philosophers possess when they have genuine knowledge of eternal forms. "Factual truths" are always contingent in the sense that there is no necessity that they exist. A major theme of Plato's *Republic* is the conflict between philosophy and politics – between philosophic truth and political opinion. Because politics is based on unstable and conflicting opinions (*doxai*), not on genuine knowledge of eternal forms, it may appear that in "real" politics power and might determine what is right and just. The *Republic* can be read as a sustained argument to refute this understanding of justice and to show that true justice can be achieved only if it meets the eternal standards of rational truth that phi-losophers aspire to know. The conflict between truth and opinion arose out of two diametrically opposed ways of life. – the life of the philosopher and the life of a citizen in a polis. To the citizen's ever-changing opinions about human affairs, the philosopher opposes the rational truth about what is everlasting, and from which principles can be derived that would stabilize human affairs. "Hence the opposite to truth was mere opinion, which was equated with illusion, and it was this degrading of opinion that gave the conflict its political poignancy; for opinion, and not truth, belongs among the indispensable prerequisites of all power" (Arendt 1977: 233).

Traces of this original conflict can still be found in the earlier stages of the modern age, but the conflict between rational truth and opinion is not the primary problem today – although there are vestiges in the current attacks on scientific truth. The idea that philosophers possess a special kind of knowledge and truth that sets the standards for politics has been ridiculed. (It was also ridiculed in Ancient Greece.) Nevertheless, there is an important lesson to be learned from the conflict of rational truth and opinion. Arendt claims that the tradition of political philosophy has always sought to impose its standards of truth on politics. Debating opinions (in her distinctive sense of "opinion") in a public space created by a plurality of human beings is the essence of politics – or rather, of what politics should be. In short, against the tradition of denigrating opinions by philosophers, Arendt celebrates the conflict of opinions as constituting the life and dignity of politics. When Arendt speaks about opinions, she does not mean what is measured by public opinion polls. Individuals do not simply "have" opinions; they *form* opinions in and through public debate.

> I form an opinion by considering a given issue from different viewpoints, by making present to my mind the standpoints of those who are absent; that is, I represent them. . . . The more people's standpoints I have present in my mind while I am pondering a given issue, and the better I can imagine how I would feel and think if I were in their place, the stronger will be the capacity for representative thinking and the more valid my final conclusions, my opinion. (Arendt 1977: 241)

The formation of opinion is not a private activity performed by solitary individuals in isolation. Opinions can be tested and enlarged only where there are *genuine* encounters with differing opinions – whether these are actual encounters or encounters achieved through imagination. There is no fixed, permanent test for the adequacy of opinions, no authority for judging them other than the better argument in public debate. This is why the formation of opinions requires a community of political equals and a willingness to submit opinions to exposure and critique. Here too is an important lesson to be learned from Arendt that has contemporary relevance. There is a dangerous tendency today to refuse to listen to others who disagree with us. We don't really want to consider different viewpoints, except to condemn or ridicule them. And this tendency is exacerbated because of the ways in which we get our "information" from sources that only reinforce our entrenched prejudices. Arendt also sharply distinguishes opinions from group interests.

Interest and opinion are entirely different political phenomena. Politically, interests are relevant only as group interests, and for the purification of such group interest it seems to suffice that they are represented in such a way that their partial character is safe-guarded under all conditions, even under the condition that the interest of one group happens to be the interest of the majority. Opinions, on the contrary, never belong to groups but exclusively to individuals who "exert their reason coolly and freely," and no multitude, be it the multitude of a part or of the whole of society, will ever be capable of forming an opinion. Opinions will rise wherever men communicate freely with one another and have the right to make their views public but these views in their endless variety seem to stand also in need of purification and representation. (Arendt 1965b: 229)

The opposite of rational truth is ignorance and error, but the opposite of factual truth is *deliberate lying*. Factual truth is far more fragile than rational truth. Because facts are contingent, because there is no necessity for facts to be true or false, it becomes much easier to deny factual truths and to eliminate them by deliberate lying. Factual truth, when it stands in the way of someone's basic convictions, encounters enormous hostility. Facts and opinions also need to be carefully distinguished. Factual truth is established by witnesses and testimony, and it exists only to the extent that it is spoken and written about. Facts should inform opinions even though opinions can differ widely as long as they respect facts. "Freedom of opinion is a farce unless factual information is guaranteed and the facts themselves are not in dispute" (Arendt 1977: 238). Unfortunately, one of the most successful techniques for denying factual truth is to claim that a so-called factual truth is just another opinion. This tendency to blur the distinction between factual truth and opinion is becoming increasingly prevalent. To illustrate the difference between facts and opinions, Arendt tells the story of the Clemenceau, who was asked his opinion concerning what future historians might say about who was responsible for the outbreak of the First World War. "He replied, 'This I do not know. But I know for certain that they will not say Belgium invaded Germany'" (Arendt 1977: 239). But even this reply displays naïveté. We know from the rewriting of history that even such brute facts as Trotsky's role in the Russian Revolution can be obliterated. What happened so blatantly in totalitarian societies is being practiced today by leading politicians. In short, there is the constant danger that powerful persuasive techniques are being used to deny factual truth, to transform fact into just another opinion, and to create a world of "alternative facts."

74

Arendt warns about an even greater danger: "[T]he result of a consistent and total substitution of lies for factual truth is not that the lies will now be accepted as truth, and truth defamed as lies, but that the sense by which we take our bearings in the real world – and the category of truth vs. falsehood is among the mental means to this end – *is being destroyed*" (Arendt 1977: 257, my emphasis). Arendt had a deep insight into something that we are living through now. The very categories of truth versus falsehood, facts versus lies, are in the process of being obliterated. Consequently, the possibilities for lying become boundless and frequently meet with little resistance. Typically, political lies were used deliberately to deceive. This still presupposes a distinction between lies and factual truth. But Arendt notes that the deceiver can come to believe his own lies. She points out how difficult it can be to lie to others without coming to believe one's lies. To make her point, she relates a medieval anecdote about what happened one night when a watchtower sentry decided to play a practical joke. He sounded an alarm to scare the townspeople about the approach of an enemy. He was overwhelmingly successful. Everybody rushed to the walls and the last to rush was the sentry himself. "The tale suggests to what an extent our apprehension of reality is dependent on sharing our world with our fellow-men, and what strength of character is required to stick to anything, truth or lie, that is unshared. In other words, the more successful the liar is, the more likely it is that he will fall prey to his own fabrications" (Arendt 1977: 254).

When confronted by a deceiver who believes his own lies or, what is worse, can no longer distinguish his lies from factual truth, we are dealing with a much more intractable phenomenon. Since the political liar is a "man of action," he seeks to change the world to conform to his lies. In the extreme case of totalitarianism, this is precisely what totalitarian leaders sought to achieve. This is a temptation and a danger that we see today in non-totalitarian societies. It is disturbing to read Arendt's description of the uses of totalitarian propaganda in light of what is occurring today throughout the world. For what is happening seems like a replay of what totalitarianism regimes carried out in a much more extreme form. People are obsessed with a desire to escape from the harsh reality of their everyday lives because of their loss of social status and the disappearance of a world that was familiar to them. It is as if a common-sense world of jobs, stability, and social advancement has collapsed. In such a fragmented and disoriented world, factual truth is no longer important. "What convinces masses are not facts, not even invented facts, but only the consistency of the system of which they are presumably a part" (Arendt 1976: 351). People who feel that they have been neglected and forgotten yearn for a narrative that will make sense of the anxiety and the misery they are experiencing – one that promises redemption from their troubles. In such a situation, an authoritarian leader can exploit the anxieties that people are experiencing and successfully blur the distinction between lies and reality. Argument and appeal to facts are not really important for such propaganda. An appealing fictional story can be foolproof against factual truth, reality, or argument.

A new form of lying has emerged in recent times. This is what Arendt calls "image-making," where factual truth is dismissed if it doesn't fit the image. The image becomes a substitute for reality. All such lies harbor an element of violence: organized lying always tends to destroy whatever it has decided to negate. The difference between the traditional political lie and the modern lie is the difference between hiding something and destroying it. We have recently seen how fabricated images can become a reality for millions of people, including the image-maker himself. We have witnessed this in the 2016 American presidential election. Despite the obvious falsity of his claims, the president insists that the crowd at his inauguration was the largest in history; despite the fact that he did not receive a majority of votes, he insists that this was because millions of fraudulent votes were cast; and despite the evidence that Russians interfered with the presidential election, the president claims that the "suggestion" that there was Russian interference is just a devious way of calling his legitimacy into question. The real danger here is that an image is created that loyal followers want to believe regardless of what is factually true. They are encouraged to dismiss anything that conflicts with the image as "fake news" or the conspiracy of elites who want to fool them. What Arendt wrote more than a half a century ago might have been written yesterday. "Contemporary history is full of instances in which tellers of factual truth were felt to be more dangerous, and even more hostile, than the real opponents" (Arendt 1977: 255). Arendt was not sanguine that tellers of factual truth would triumph over image-makers. Factual truth-telling is frequently powerless against image-making and can be defeated in a head-on clash with the powers that be. Nevertheless, she did think that ultimately factual truth has a stubborn power of its own. Image-makers know this, and that is why they seek to discredit a free press and institutions where there is a pursuit of impartial truth.

Thus far I have been focusing on the power of lying by an authoritarian leader – one who comes to believe his own lies; but there is another variation on lying that becomes obsessed with images. Arendt discusses this in her essay "Lying in Politics," her response to the public revelation of the "top secret" document, *The Pentagon Papers*. In June 1967, Robert S. McNamara, the secretary of defense, commissioned a forty-seven-volume "History of U.S. Decision Making Process of Vietnam Policy." In 1971, Daniel Ellsberg, who participated in writing the report, leaked this richly documented history of the American role in Indochina. Selections were published in *The New York Times* and *The Washington Post*.

The basic issue raised by the publication of *The Pentagon Papers* was deception – systematic and consistent lying to the American people by government authorities. Lying pervaded the ranks of all government services, military and civilian – "the phony body counts of the 'search and destroy' missions, the doctored after-damage reports of the Air Force, the 'progress' reports to Washington from the field written by subordinates who knew that their performance would be evaluated by their own reports" (Arendt 1972: 4). This was lying on a grand scale, in which all sorts of people throughout the government were complicit. It is precisely the fragility and contingency of facts that makes "deception so easy *up to a point*, and so tempting. It never comes into conflict with reason because things could indeed have been as the liar maintains they were. Lies are often much more plausible, more appealing than reason, than reality, because the liar has the great advantage of knowing beforehand what the audience wishes or expects to hear" (Arendt 1972: 6). The liar has prepared his story for public consumption with a careful eye to making it plausible – more plausible than factual reality.

What is so striking about *The Pentagon Papers* is that, while this image-making was taking place, the intelligence community was supplying accurate factual information that contradicted the image created. But this factual information was simply ignored or denied. It was ignored by intelligent "problem-solvers" who substituted all sorts of "scenarios" for factual truth. What these "problem-solvers" have in common with down-to-earth liars is the attempt to get rid of facts. They had a (false) sense of their own omnipotence. They became obsessed with the image itself – the image of the United States as the greatest power on earth. 'Image-making as a global policy – not world conquest but the victory 'to win people's minds' – is indeed something new in the huge arsenal of human follies recorded in history" (Arendt 1972: 18). The question that arises is: How could this happen? How could the "problem-solvers" so completely ignore the factual reality of what was happening on the ground? The "problem-solvers" and "decision-makers" came to believe their own lies. Arendt notes that there was a new twist here. It is as if the normal process of self-deception was reversed; deception did not end up with self-deception, but rather self-deception came *first*.

The deceivers started with self-deception. Probably because of their high station and their astounding self-assurance, they were so convinced of overwhelming success, not on the battlefield, but in the public-relations arena, and so certain of their psychological premises about the unlimited possibilities of manipulating people, that they *anticipated* general belief and victory in the battle for people's minds. And since they lived in a defactualized world anyway, they did not find it difficult to pay no more attention to the fact that their audience refused to be convinced than to other facts. (Arendt 1972: 35)

Arendt leaves us with an ambiguous conclusion. On the one hand, she claims that there are no limits to organized lying, image-making, deception, and self-deception. On the other hand, despite the seeming impotence of truth-tellers in the face of overwhelming power, there comes a point at which systematic political lying begins to break down. Political lying can destroy factual truth, but it can never replace it. Arendt teaches us how effective and dangerous political lying and image-making can be. It is naïve to believe that insisting on factual truth can challenge the power of lies. This underestimates the sophistication of image-makers in denigrating, mocking, and destroying factual truth. It underestimates the extent to which political liars will claim that a free press is the source of "fake news." She notes the danger of what happens when the very distinction between truth and falsehood is called into question, when people no longer care about what is a lie and what is factually true. We are confronting all of these tendencies today, not only in the United States but throughout the world. Arendt would certainly be critical of those who make facile comparisons between the world today and totalitarian regimes. But what is frightening – and should serve as a *warning* – are all those similarities between organizing lying, fictional image-making, deception, and self-deception that are so prevalent today and the techniques perfected by totalitarian regimes.

Plurality, Politics, and Public Freedom

In the conclusion of her essay "Truth and Politics" Arendt writes that because she has dealt with politics from the perspective of lying,

[I] have failed to mention even in passing the greatness and the dignity of what goes on inside it. I have spoken as though the political realm were no more than a battlefield of partial, conflicting interests, where nothing counted but pleasure and profit, partisanship, and the lust for dominion. In short, I have dealt with politics as though I too believed that all public affairs were ruled by interest and power, that there would be no political realm at all if we were not bound to take care of life's necessities. (Arendt 1977: 263)

Arendt certainly had a realistic understanding of the lying, deception, self-deception, and violence that characterized politics during her lifetime – and continues to persist. She certainly was not innocent or sentimental. Politics, she once said, is not a nursery. She brilliantly analyzed the unprecedented character of totalitarianism, but at the same time she wanted to recover the dignity of politics. Today, when there is so much suspicion of politicians, it is difficult to resist becoming cynical about any and all forms of politics. Arendt did not believe in blueprints for political action. But she did believe, like the pearl-diver in Shakespeare's *Tempest,* that one can recover pearls and corals from the ruins and fragments of the past that might shed illumination on what politics once was – and might still yet become. Her positive conception of politics provides a critical standard for judging what is lacking in politics today. This is another reason why Arendt should be read now.

Many commentators and critics of Arendt think that she first laid out her positive conception of politics in *The Human Condition* (1958a). Because she relies so heavily on an idealized conception of the Greek polis and the Roman republic, she has been criticized for developing a conception of politics that is irrelevant today. But I believe that this criticism is mistaken. The starting point for her thinking about politics was neither the Greeks nor the Romans, but her personal experience. We have seen anticipations of this in her discussion of statelessness and refugees, the right to have rights, and the calamity of the rightless. Recall that she declared that it was the loss of a polity – the loss of a community willing to guarantee and protect rights of individuals – that deprives human beings of their humanity. In her defense of a Jewish homeland in Palestine, her advocacy of local Arab–Jewish councils organized into a federated state, we also see the seeds of her positive conception of politics. But, most significantly, it was dwelling on the horrors of totalitarianism, and discerning the final aim of total domination – the destruction of human individuality, spontaneity, and plurality – that oriented her search for the meaning of politics. Claude Lefort's comment on the basis of Arendt's thinking about politics is illuminating.

> Arendt's reading of totalitarianism in both its Nazi and Stalinist version governs the subsequent elaboration of her theory of politics. She conceptualizes politics by inverting the image of totalitarianism and this leads her to look not for a model of politics – the use of the term "model" would betray her intentions – but for a reference to politics in certain privileged moments when its features are most clearly discernible: the moments of the American and French Revolutions. The moment of the workers' councils in Russia in 1917 and that of the Hungarian councils of 1956 might also be added to the list. (Lefort 1988: 50)

Lefort captures the spirit of Arendt's recovery of the dignity of politics when he writes that she was

86

searching for those "privileged moments when its distinctive features were most clearly discernible." This is the spirit in which she approached the Greek polis and the Roman republic, the American and French Revolutions, and the outbreaks of what she called "the revolutionary spirit" from the eighteenth century until the present.

I want to explore the intricate network of concepts that Arendt interweaves in order to texture the meaning and dignity of politics: action, plurality, natality, speech, appearance, public space, public freedom, power (empowerment), persuasion, and political judgment. We need to pay close attention to Arendt's distinctive use of these concepts. Thinking requires making careful distinctions in order to illuminate fundamental issues. In *The Human Condition* Arendt analyzes what she calls the *Vita Activa* (the active life), which has traditionally been contrasted with the *Vita Comtemplativa* (the contemplative life). She distinguishes three different types of activity that comprise the *Vita Activa*: labor, work, and action. Labor is the type of activity that is required for human survival. Unless humans satisfy their bodily needs they will not survive. Work is the type of activity involved in creating an artificial world where life can be stabilized – a world that has some durability and permanence. Action (in Arendt's distinctive sense) is the only activity that takes place directly between human beings without an intermediary; it corresponds to the human condition of plurality. "While all aspects of the human condition are somehow related to politics, this plurality is specifically *the* condition – not only the *conditio sine qua non*, but *the conditio per quam* – of all political life" (Arendt 1958: 7).

There are many important questions that can be raised about Arendt's controversial distinction between labor and work, but I want to concentrate on action – the activity that stands at the heart of politics. What does Arendt mean when she asserts that action corresponds to the human condition of plurality? Plurality signifies that each of us has a distinctive perspective on the world. We can express this distinction and distinguish ourselves by communicating who we are in public. Speech and action reveal this distinctiveness of who we are. Action, for Arendt, is the capacity to initiate, to begin something new. Every human being has this capacity, even though it may lie dormant, be suppressed, or even destroyed by total domination. "Action and speech are so closely related because the primordial and specifically human act must at the same time contain an answer to the question asked of every newcomer: 'Who are you?' This disclosure of who somebody is, is implicit in both his words and deeds" (Arendt 1958a: 178).

Action is also grounded in natality – "the new beginning inherent in birth can make itself felt in the world only because the newcomer possesses the capacity to begin something anew, that is, acting" (Arendt 1958a: 9). Natality, of course, refers to birth, but Arendt underscores a "second birth" whereby we bring about a new beginning. Although she stresses the human capacity to begin, to initiate, to set in motion something new, we do not act in isolation. We act in *concert* with our fellow human beings and reveal who we are as distinctive individuals. One of Arendt's most original conceptions is the idea of public spaces. Public spaces do not exist naturally; they need to be artificially created by human beings. These are the spaces in which we act, speak, form and test opinions, in debating with one another. Strictly speaking, politics arises *between* human beings. Arendt also highlights the affinity between politics and the performing arts. "Performing artists – dancers, play-actors, musicians, and the like – need an audience to show their virtuosity, just as acting men need the presence of others before whom they can appear; both need a publicly organized space for their 'work,' and both depend on others for the performance itself" (Arendt 1977: 154).

Arendt draws upon the Greek concept of isonomy – political equality – to elucidate politics. Traditionally, the basic political questions have been who rules over whom, what are the different types of rulership, and what are the sources of their legitimacy. But Arendt conceives of politics in a much more radical fashion. Politics is a form of *no rule*; politics does not involve one individual or group ruling over others. Rather, political equality is essential for politics; we debate and act among our peers. Individuals are not born equal: they have different abilities and talents. Isonomy in the Greek polis "guaranteed . . . equality, but not because all men were born or created equal but, on the contrary, because men were by nature . . . not equal, and needed an artificial institution, the polis, which by virtue of its laws [*nomos*] would make them equal . . .

The equality of the Greek polis, its isonomy, was an attribute of the polis and not of men, who received their equality by virtue of citizenship, not by virtue of birth" (Arendt 1965b: 23). In the Greek polis, no one could be free except among his peers. In the polis freedom exists only among political equals.

> The reason for this insistence on the interconnection of freedom and equality in Greek political thought was that freedom was understood as being manifest in certain, by no means all, human activities, and that these activities could appear and be real only when others saw them, judged them, remembered them. The life of a free man needed the presence of others. Freedom itself needed therefore a place where people could come together – the agora, the market-place or the polis, the political space proper. (Arendt 1965b: 24)

In probing the meaning of isonomy and freedom in the Greek polis, Arendt is highlighting an essential feature of the dignity of *all* genuine politics. She is fleshing out what she first sketched in her discussion of the "right to have rights" – the idea of a polity and public spaces where individuals can act, deliberate, and be judged by their actions and opinions. This interweaving of the concepts of action, natality, plurality, and public spaces sets the context for a further examination of tangible worldly public freedom.

In her essay "What is Freedom?" Arendt distinguishes between the philosophical problem of freedom, which deals with the question of inward free will, and the political idea of public worldly freedom. She argues that public freedom existed in the Greek polis long before thinkers such as St. Augustine struggled with the problem of free will. The philosophical issue of free will emerged when public freedom began to disappear. For Arendt, the *raison d'être* of politics is freedom and its field of experience in action in the political realm. Without a politically guaranteed public realm, freedom lacks the public space to make its appearance. To clarify what she means by public freedom, Arendt draws not only upon the isonomy of the Greek polis but also upon the characterization of public worldly freedom by the *philosophes* of the eighteenth century.

Their public freedom was not an inner realm into which men might escape at will from the pressures of the world, nor was it the *liberum arbitrium* which makes the will choose between alternatives. Freedom for them could exist only in public, it was a tangible, worldly reality, something created by men to be enjoyed by men rather than a gift or a capacity, it was the man-made public space of the market-place which antiquity had known as the area where freedom appears and becomes visible to all. (Arendt 1965b: 120–1)

Like the pearl-diver, Arendt reaches back to the Greeks and the *philosophes* of the eighteenth century to recover what *is* (not merely what *was*) worldly tangible public freedom – the type of freedom that totalitarian regimes sought to destroy. This is the public freedom that was exhibited by the Founding Fathers in their public debates about founding a new republic. And this is the public tangible freedom that has come alive in every manifestation of the revolutionary spirit, from the eighteenth century through the Budapest uprising of 1956. Public freedom is a *positive* worldly achievement that arises when a plurality of human beings act and debate in public spaces, share and test opinions, and seek to persuade one another.

Arendt also carefully distinguishes public freedom from liberation. Liberation is always liberation *from* something or someone – whether it is liberation from the misery of poverty or from oppressive rulers. The distinction that Arendt draws between public freedom and liberation is one of her most important distinctions, and it is relevant to contemporary politics, where there is a tendency to fuse or confuse liberation and freedom. Consider, for example, one of the key claims that the Bush administration employed to justify the 2003 military intervention in Iraq. The American public was led to believe that with the overthrow of Saddam Hussein, freedom would flourish in Iraq and spread throughout the Middle East. We now know that this was a disastrous illusion. Liberation from oppressors may be a *necessary* condition for freedom, but it is never a *sufficient* condition for the achievement of positive public freedom. The overthrow of tyrants, dictators, and totalitarian leaders does not by itself bring about positive tangible freedom. This is a bitter lesson that must be learned over and over again. Even now in the war against ISIS, there is certainly no guarantee that "military victory" will bring about public freedom in the region.

There is another reason why Arendt's distinction between public freedom and liberation is important. Many liberal and libertarian thinkers identify freedom with negative liberty. We are presumably free when we minimize or eliminate any "coercion" by the state or government. These thinkers are deeply suspicious of the idea of positive public freedom, because they think it leads us down the slippery slope to oppression and even totalitarianism. What is so impressive about Arendt's characterization of public freedom is that it stands in opposition to all forms of authoritarian oppression and domination. On the contrary, she developed her idea of public freedom as an answer to authoritarian rule and totalitarianism.

We can deepen our grasp of Arendt's conception of politics when we see how it is related to her understanding of power, which she contrasts with violence. In her essay "On Violence" Arendt cites C. Wright Mills, who starkly affirms: "All politics is a struggle for power. And the ultimate kind of power is violence." This declaration echoes "Max Weber's definition of the state as 'the rule of men over men based on the means of legitimate, that is allegedly legitimate violence'"

(Arendt 1970: 35). This well-entrenched popular paradigm of power has a long history; power is taken to mean the rule of an individual, group, or state *over* others; it involves command and obedience. If this is the way in which one conceives of power, then it makes perfect sense to claim that the ultimate kind of power is violence. Arendt well understood this traditional concept of power. In *The Origins* she argues that totalitarian regimes carry it to its utmost extreme. But Arendt, in her endeavor to defend the dignity of politics, criticizes this prevailing idea of power. Power and violence are not only distinguishable; they are *antithetical* concepts. Where true politics reigns, there is rational persuasion, not violence. And when violence reigns, it destroys power.

> Power corresponds to the human ability not just to act but to act in concert. Power is never the property of an individual: it belongs to a group and remains in existence only so long as the group keeps together. When we say of somebody that he is "in power" we actually refer to his being empowered by a certain number of people to act in their name. The moment the group from which power originated to begin with (*potestas in populo*,

without a people or group there is no power) disappears, "his power" also vanishes. (Arendt 1970: 44)

Let us analyze this passage carefully. We have seen that to act is not to act alone but to act in concert with our fellow human beings in public spaces that we have mutually created. Power is what makes acting in concert possible. Consequently, unlike strength, which may be a characteristic of a single individual, power is never an attribute of a single individual; it is an attribute of the group that acts in concert. This is similar to the way in which Arendt speaks of isonomy, which is an attribute of a political community, not of single individuals.

The next point is extremely important. The power of a group exists only as long as the group acts together. When political groups dissolve or fall apart, then their power disappears. When Arendt speaks of someone "in power," she is referring to political leadership. The person in power does not *rule over* members of the group. He is empowered by them, and they can always withdraw their power from the person (or group) empowered. What is striking about Arendt's conception of power (and her understanding of politics) is that it is not to be understood in a vertical, hierarchical manner, where it means the control of one individual or group *over* another. Power is a horizontal concept: it springs up and grows when a plurality of individuals act together and treat each other as political equals.

> [P]ower comes into being only if and when men join themselves for the purpose of action, and it will disappear when, for whatever reason, they disperse and desert one another. Hence, binding and promising, combining and covenanting, are the means by which power is kept in existence; where and when men succeed in keeping intact the power that sprang up between them during the course of any particular act or deed, they are also in the process of foundation, of constituting a stable worldly structure to house, as it were, their combined power of action. (Arendt 1965b: 174)

Given this conception of power and empowerment that is created when human beings act together, we can understand why Arendt claims that power and violence are antithetical. Violence is essentially anti-political. It uses tools, weapons, and sophisticated technological devices to destroy power. "Violence can destroy power: out of the barrel of a gun grows the most effective command resulting in instant and perfect obedience. What can never grow out of it is power" (Arendt 1970: 53). Furthermore, when existing regimes begin to lose their power, they resort to violence. But just as violence can destroy power, power can overwhelm violence. We witnessed this effectiveness of power as empowerment not only with Gandhi and the American civil rights movement, but also in the movements that sprang up throughout Eastern Europe and led to the overthrow of communist regimes. In each of these cases, we have examples of the growth and effectiveness of nonviolent power. Arendt, of course, is aware that in the "real" world we normally find a combination of violence and power. Nevertheless, it is politically important to distinguish carefully between power as empowerment and violence. She seeks to capture something that is quintessential about empowerment and public tangible freedom.

To round out Arendt's thick description of politics – a description intended to show the dignity of politics – I want to discuss the role of persuasion and judgment in politics. Throughout her analysis of politics, Arendt stresses the close connection between action and speech. The type of speech that is so fundamental to politics is where we seek to persuade our fellow human beings with whom we share a common world. Persuasion involves free open debate and argument with our peers and the exercise of judgment. In her essay, "The Crisis of Culture," Arendt makes the striking claim that in the first part of Kant's *Critique of Judgment*, where Kant explicitly deals with aesthetic judgment, we actually find Kant's unwritten political philosophy. She has in mind Kant's analysis of reflective judgments, the mode of thinking about particulars, which does not subsume particulars under some universal rule. Judgment involves discrimination and discerning what is distinctive about the particular situation that one confronts. Judgment requires an "enlarged mentality" wherein one exercises imagination so as to be able to think in the place of everybody else.

[T]he judging person – as Kant says quite beautifully – can only "woo the consent of everyone else" in the hope of coming to agreement with him eventually. This "wooing" or persuading corresponds closely to what the Greeks called [*peithein*], the convincing and persuading speech which they regarded as the typically political form of people talking with one another. Persuasion ruled the intercourse of the citizens of the polis because it excluded physical violence. (Arendt 1977: 222)

Kant was particularly insightful in basing judgment on the faculty of taste, but taste is not to be identified with private subjective feelings. Taste in based on the *sensus communis* – a sense that fits us into human community.

In citing Kant, Arendt is advancing her own understanding of judgment – a distinctive mode of thinking that is neither an expression of subjective feeling nor a universality characteristic of pure reasoning; it is a mode of thinking that deals with particular situations in their particularity. And this type of thinking is essential for politics. Many of the key characteristics of Arendt's conception of political judgment are summed up in the following passage.

The power of judgment rests on a potential agreement with others, and the thinking process which is active in judging something is not, like the process of pure reasoning, a dialogue between me and myself, but finds itself always and primarily, even when I am quite alone in making up my mind, in an anticipated communication with others with whom I know I must finally come to agreement. From this potential agreement judgment derives its specific validity. This means, on the one hand, that such judgment must liberate itself from the "subjective private conditions," that is, from the idiosyncrasies which naturally determine the outlook of each individual in his privacy and are legitimate as long as they are only privately held opinions, but which are not fit to enter the market place, and lack all validity in the public realm. And this enlarged way of thinking, which as judgment knows how to transcend its own individual limitations, on the other hand, cannot function in strict isolation or solitude; it needs the presence of others "in whose place" it must think, whose perspectives it must take into consideration, and without whom it never has the opportunity to operate at all. (Arendt 1977: 220)

I have sought to develop an account of Arendt's account of the meaning and dignity of politics by exploring the interdependence and the interweaving of the concepts of action, plurality, natality, speech, public spaces, isonomy, tangible public freedom, power, opinion, persuasion, and judgment. Arendt knew that when she spoke about what "politics really is" or "what politics means" she was contrasting her analysis with the common understanding of politics today. She felt strongly that the "atrophy of the political realm is one of those objectively demonstrable tendencies of the modern era" (Arendt 2003: 155). The question that needs to be raised is: How is her analysis of the meaning and dignity of politics relevant to us today? I want to answer this in several steps. First, I want to show that Arendt's conception of politics is not "merely" theoretical. I will examine what she took to be one of the exemplary privileged moments when politics was practiced – the American Revolution. Secondly, I want to explore what Arendt means by "the revolutionary spirit." Thirdly, I will show how Arendt provides us with a critical perspective for judging the failures of contemporary politics and provides a source of inspiration for political action.

The American Revolution and the Revolutionary Spirit

Arendt's most detailed discussion of a paradigmatic example of politics is the American

Revolution. In *On Revolution* she analyzes the modern meaning of revolution and draws a sharp contrast between the American and the French Revolutions. Revolution in the modern sense is not to be confused or identified with rebellion. There has been a long history of rebellions that aim at liberation from tyrants and oppressors. But the modern idea of revolution that emerges in the eighteenth century involves both liberation and freedom – and by freedom Arendt means the public tangible freedom elaborated in her conception of politics. The end of rebellion is liberation, but the end of revolution is the foundation of freedom. Although both the American and the French Revolutions started in this way, Arendt argues that the French Revolution was overwhelmed by the "social question" – the misery of mass poverty that eventually led to violence and the Terror. There was certainly poverty and slavery in the American colonies, but it was obscured and hidden; it wasn't comparable to the extreme situation in France. Unlike the French, who had suffered under absolute monarchy and had no real experience of the practices of self-government, the American colonies had experienced a long tradition of self-government, going back to the Mayflower Compact.

Originally, the American colonists, in their opposition to British rule, wanted to *restore* their rights as Englishmen; they were not revolutionaries. "[T]he acts and deeds that liberation demanded from them threw them into public business, where, intentionally or more often unexpectedly, they began to constitute that space of appearances where freedom can unfold its charms and become a visible, tangible reality" (Arendt 1965b: 26). The war of liberation from the British is not what constitutes the heart of the revolution. Rather, the Founding Fathers gained awareness that they were in the process of creating something new, founding a new body politic, a new republic that had never existed before. This revolutionary spirit was expressed in the fever of constitution-making that emerged almost as soon as the colonies declared their independence: "For in America the armed uprising of the colonies and the Declaration of Independence had been followed by the spontaneous outbreak of constitution-making – as though, in John Adams's words, 'thirteen clocks had struck as one' – so that there existed no gap, no hiatus, hardly a breathing spell between the war of liberation, the fight for independence which was the condition for freedom, and the constitution of the new states" (Arendt 1965b: 139–40).

Unlike many historians who identify the American Revolution with the war of liberation, Arendt emphasizes that the truly revolutionary element is to be identified with constitution-making. "Constitution" is an equivocal term. It can mean the act of constituting or the laws of government that are constituted. The process and the result are both important, but Arendt emphasizes the *act of constituting*. This is where debate, deliberation, contesting, and sharing of opinions takes place; this is where public freedom is manifested. She endorses Thomas Paine's definition, which sums up the American experience of constitution-making: "A constitution is not the act of government but of a people constituting a government" (Arendt 1965b: 143). Public freedom made its appearance when the colonies wrote their own state constitutions and again when the federal Constitution was drafted in Philadelphia. The draft of the Constitution required ratification by at least nine colonies. In specially convened state assemblies, the merits and defects of the new

Constitution were debated vigorously. No question preoccupied the drafters of the Constitution more than the separation of powers and the balance of power between the states and the federal government. The true objective of the American Constitution was not to limit power but to create new power – not power over, but empowerment of a federal government. This, of course, was combined with the Bill of Rights, which was designed to limit the abuse of power by the new government. The American Constitution finally consolidated the power of the Revolution. The combination of limited government, separation of powers, balancing power between the states and an empowered federal government, was the unique achievement of the American Revolution.

This brief sketch of the American Revolution exemplifies what Arendt takes to be distinctive about the dignity of politics. The Founders were acting in concert to create a new polity, a new republic. They were empowering a new form of government. Although there was a long tradition of local self-government, the Founders created new public spaces in which they could appear and argue with each other. They viewed this not as a burden but as a joy in experiencing their public freedom, what they called "public happiness." The Founders had many sharp and bitter differences, but they nevertheless treated each other as political equals. They were engaged in vigorous argument and persuasion. When necessary, they compromised. Violence was, of course, involved in the war of liberation, but violence plays *no* role in the revolutionary achievement of creating a new republic. The American Revolution is one of the privileged moments in history when the meaning and dignity of politics is concretely manifested.

Arendt celebrates the American Revolution and speaks of its "success," but she is extremely critical of what happened *after* the ratification of the Constitution. There was a failure to remember and to understand conceptually what was distinctive about the revolutionary spirit. There was also a failure to provide it with a lasting political institution. No space was reserved for the exercise of the very qualities that had led to the founding of the republic. There was a deep perplexity that seemed unresolvable. "This perplexity, namely, that the principle of public freedom and public happiness without which no revolution would ever have come to pass should remain the privilege of the generation of founders" (Arendt

1965b: 235). The problem was how to create stable and enduring political institutions such that the public freedom and public happiness that were so cherished by the revolutionary Founders could continue to flourish. Thomas Jefferson was the person who most acutely recognized and struggled with this issue. He felt that even though the Revolution had given freedom to the people, it had nevertheless failed to create political institutions where this freedom could continue to be exercised by succeeding generations. "Only the representatives of the people, not the people themselves, had an opportunity to engage in those activities of 'expressing, discussing, and deciding' which in a positive sense are the activities of freedom" (Arendt 1965b: 238).

Late in his career, Jefferson proposed a system of local wards or "elementary republics" in which the people themselves, not just their representatives, could express their public freedom. This was not a complete novelty in America; it had been practiced in town meetings in which local citizens directly participated in their self-government. Jefferson's great fear was that without such active "elementary republics" the spirit of public freedom would wither away.

Jefferson himself knew well enough that what he proposed as the "salvation of the republic" actually was the salvation of the revolutionary spirit through the republic. His expositions of the ward system always began with a reminder of how "the vigor given to our revolution in its commencement" was due to the "little republics," how they had "thrown the whole nation into energetic action," and how, at a later occasion, he had felt "the foundations of the government shaken under [his] feet by the New England townships," "the energy of this organization" being so great that "there was not an individual in their States whose body was not thrown with all its momentum into action." Hence, he expected the wards to permit the citizens to continue to do what they had been able to do during the years of revolution, namely, to act on their own and thus to participate in public business as it was being transacted from day to day. (Arendt 1965b: 254)

In citing Jefferson, Arendt is speaking in her *own* voice – not just about the American Revolution, but about the spontaneous outbreak of the revolutionary spirit ever since the eighteenth century. These revolutions created "islands of freedom"

(Arendt 1977: 6). In each instance there was a spontaneous creation of councils by the people themselves. She cites the examples of the French *societés revolutionnaires*, the Paris Commune of 1871, the Russian *soviets* created in 1905 and again in 1917, and the *Räte* that emerged in the Spartacus uprising in Germany as manifestations of the revolutionary spirit. Each time these councils appeared, they sprang up as the spontaneous organs of the people, and they were also quickly destroyed – frequently by "professional revolutionaries." She felt that this rare creation of an "island of freedom" sprang up once again in the French *résistance*. Suddenly, once again "without premonition and probably against their conscious intentions," the participants in the *résistance* constituted "willy-nilly a public realm where – without the paraphernalia of officialdom and hidden from the eyes of friend and foe – all relevant business in the affairs of the country was transacted in deed and word" (Arendt 1977: 3). One of Arendt's favorite French poets and writers was René Char, who particpated in the the French *résistance*. She frequently cited his aphorism "*Notre héritage n'est précédé d'aucun testament*" (our inheritance was left to us by no testament). Arendt interpreted this as referring to "the lost treasure" of the tangible freedom that the participants of the *résistance* had experienced.

Despite Arendt's warnings about the subterranean elements that crystallized in totalitarianism, many of which still exist today, she also claimed that the history of revolutions from the summer of 1776 in the U.S. and the summer of 1789 in Paris to the autumn of 1956 in Budapest – politically spells out the innermost story of the modern age. Yet this story "could be told in parable form as a tale of an age-old treasure which appears abruptly, unexpectedly and disappears again, under different mysterious circumstances, as though it were a fata morgana" (Arendt 1977: 5). It is this "lost treasure" that Arendt wants to recover in order to keep alive its memory. But not simply as a memory of something that happened in the past, but rather as naming a real possibility that is rooted in our natality, our capacity to act, to initiate, to begin something new.

Arendt's most enthusiastic and vivid description of the outbreak of the revolutionary spirit and the emergence of the council system is her essay on the Budapest uprising of 1956. Although it only lasted for twelve days and was crushed by

Soviet tanks, it nevertheless exhibited the exhila-
rating experience of people acting together and
creating their own public freedom. There was
the spontaneous creation of revolutionary and
workers' councils, "the same organization which
for more than a hundred years now has emerged
whenever people have been permitted for a few
days, or a few weeks or months, to follow their
own political devices without a government (or
a party program) imposed from above" (Arendt
1958a: 497).

In Hungary, we have seen the simultaneous
setting-up of all kinds of councils, each of them cor-
responding to a previously existing group in which
people habitually lived together or met regularly
and knew each other. Thus neighborhood councils
emerged from sheer living together and grew into
county and other territorial councils; revolutionary
councils grew out of fighting together; councils of
writers and artists, one is tempted to think, were
born in *cafés*, students' and youths' councils at the
university, military councils in the army, councils
of civil servants in ministries, workers' councils in
factories, and so on. The formation of a council in
each disparate group turned a merely haphazard

togetherness into a political institution. (Arendt 1958b: 500)

For all Arendt's praise of the council system, I don't think that she ever solved the problem that so worried Jefferson – how to find a stable enduring political institution that would house the revolutionary spirit. Whenever the councils spontaneously emerged, they were quickly destroyed. But she captures something important about the spirit of these councils that is still relevant for us today. She gives expression to what many people deeply feel today when she writes:

The councils say: We want to participate, we want to debate, we want our voices heard in public, and we want to have a possibility to determine the political course of our country. Since the country is too big for all of us to come together and determine our fate, we need a number of public spaces within it. The booth in which we deposit our ballots is unquestionably too small, for this booth has room for only one. The parties are completely unsuitable; there we are, most of us, nothing but the manipulated electorate. But if only ten of us are sitting around a table, each expressing his opinion, each hearing the opinions of others, then a rational formation of opinion can take place through the exchange of opinions. (Arendt 1972: 232–3)

Arendt expresses what was always fundamental for her and should be fundamental for us – the desire of people to have their voices heard in public, to become genuine participants in shaping their political life. She sought to recover and to conceptualize the revolutionary spirit wherein public freedom becomes a living reality. Arendt had an acute sense of the prevailing tendencies in modern society that undermine, distort, and suppress politics and public freedom. But she never gave up her conviction in the power of the revolutionary spirit to burst forth again. In her own lifetime, she saw it come alive in the Budapest uprising of 1956 and in the early days of the Civil Rights movement in the United States. If she had lived to see the emergence of the political movements that spread across Eastern and Central Europe in the 1980s, she would have cited them as further evidence of the power of the revolutionary spirit – the power that springs forth when individuals act together. These were movements that began with small groups of people sitting around tables, debating and sharing opinions. Leaders of these movements, such as Adam Michnik in Poland, drew their inspiration from the writings of Arendt. What makes Arendt so relevant today is the combination of her dire warnings about prevailing tendencies in society that are so like those that crystalized in totalitarianism together with her deep conviction about the possibility of people coming together and acting in concert, exercising their public freedom and changing the course of history.

Personal and Political Responsibility

Responsibility is a theme, in its many variations, that runs throughout the life and work of Hannah Arendt. In her personal life, we have seen how, when she escaped from Germany in 1933, she made the decision to take on the responsibility of engaging in practical work to oppose the Nazis. In the early 1940s, she argued that the Jewish people should assume responsibility for forming an international army to join with others in the fight against Hitler. When she believed that extreme ideology was taking over the Zionist movement and ignoring the complexities of the

Arab–Jewish problem in Palestine, she felt it was her responsibility to dissent. After the end of the Second World War, she discussed other aspects of responsibility. She was highly critical of the Adenauer administration in Germany for its reluctance to single out and put on trial former Nazis who had been murderers. She strongly objected to the idea of collective guilt. It obscured the distinction between those who were really responsible and guilty of murder and others who supported the regime tacitly. "Where all are guilty, nobody in the last analysis can be judged" (Arendt 1994: 126). The Eichmann trial raised further questions about responsibility. Arendt criticized the excuses that were made in Eichmann's defense – that he was simply follow-ing orders, that he was carrying out his duties as an SS officer, that he was a cog in a vast bureau-cratic machine. She also objected to the inflated (and mistaken idea) that Eichmann alone was responsible for the Final Solution. She believed that in a legal trial an *individual* is on trial – not a bureaucratic system – and the task of the judges was to judge whether Eichmann was guilty and responsible for his criminal deeds. The judges rec-ognized the distinctiveness of Eichmann's crimes when they asserted that the extent to which a criminal was "close to or remote from the actual killer means nothing, as far as responsibility is concerned. On the contrary, in general *the degree of responsibility increases as we draw farther away from the man who uses the fatal instrument with his own hands*" (Arendt 1965a: 247, italics original).

The deepest theme concerning responsibility that runs through all her thinking – and is so relevant today – is the need to take responsibility for our political lives. Arendt was ruthlessly critical of all explicit or implicit appeals to historical necessity. Because of our natality, our action, our capacity to initiate, we can always begin something new. Arendt rejected both reckless optimism and reckless despair. She was equally critical of the belief that there is a hidden logic of history that will inevitably result in the triumph of freedom and the belief that there is a hidden logic to history whereby everything is going downhill. Progress and Doom are two sides of the same coin; they are both articles of superstition. She resisted both false hope and false despair. She was bold in describing the darkness of our times – lying, deception, self-deception, image-making, and the attempt to obliterate the very distinction between truth and falsehood. She constantly warned about all those dangerous tendencies in contemporary life that still exist and haunt us. She also warned about giving in to despair and cynicism. Her exploration of the meaning and dignity of politics was intended to be an act of retrieval and recovery – a reminder of a real possibility rooted in our natality. She wanted to keep alive the revolutionary spirit – the spontaneous creation of spaces of tangible, worldly, public freedom. She was keenly aware of the disparity between her conception of politics and the ways in which we normally think of politics today. She certainly did not intend her description of politics to be a blueprint for action. But her defense of the dignity of politics does become a critical standard for *judging* what is so lacking in our contemporary politics, where there is so little opportunity genuinely to participate, to act in concert, and to debate with our peers. We must resist the temptation to opt out of politics, to assume that nothing can be done in the face of all its current ugliness and corruption. To do so is to allow ourselves to become complicit with the worst. Arendt's life-long project was to understand, to comprehend, and to do this in a way that honestly confronts both the darkness of our times *and* the sources of illumination. What she says about comprehension at the beginning of *The Origins* is what she sought to do throughout her life.

> Comprehension does not mean denying the outrageous, deducing the unprecedented from precedents, or explaining phenomena by such analogies and generalizations that the impact of reality and the shock of experience are no longer felt. It means, rather, examining and bearing consciously the burden our century has placed on us – neither denying its existence nor submitting meekly to its weight. Comprehension, in short, means the unpremeditated, attentive facing up to, and resisting of reality – whatever it may be. (Arendt 1976: viii)

The task she set herself is now *our* task – to bear the burden of *our* century and neither to deny its existence nor submit meekly to its weight. Arendt should be read today because she so was so perceptive in comprehending the dangers that still confront us and warned us about becoming indifferent or cynical. She urged us to take responsibility for our political destinies. She taught us that we have the capacity to act in concert, to initiate, to begin, to strive to make freedom a worldly reality. "Beginning, before it becomes a historical event, is the supreme capacity of man: politically it is identical with man's freedom" (Arendt 1976: 479).

Works Cited

Allen, D. S. (2004) *Talking to Strangers.* Chicago: University of Chicago Press.

Arendt, H. (1958a) *The Human Condition.* Chicago: University of Chicago Press.

—— (1958b) *The Origins of Totalitarianism,* 2nd edn. New York: Meridian Books.

—— (1959) "Reflections on Little Rock." *Dissent* 6. 1: 45–56.

—— (1965a) *Eichmann in Jerusalem: A Report on the Banality of Evil,* 2nd edn. New York: Penguin Books.

—— (1965b) *On Revolution.* New York: Viking Press.

—— (1968) *Men in Dark Times.* New York: Harcourt Brace & World.

—— (1970) *On Violence*. New York: Harcourt, Inc.

—— (1971) "Thinking and Moral Considerations." *Social Research* 38. 3: 417–46.

—— (1972) *Crises of the Republic*. New York: Harcourt Brace Jovanovich.

—— (1976) *The Origins of Totalitarianism*, new edition with added prefaces. New York: Harcourt, Inc.

—— (1977) *Between Past and Future*. New York: Penguin Books.

—— (1994) *Essays in Understanding*, ed. J. Kohn. Harcourt Brace & Co.

—— (2003) *The Promise of Politics*, ed. J. Kohn. New York: Schocken Books.

—— (2007) *The Jewish Writings*, ed. J. Kohn and R. H. Feldman. New York: Schocken Books.

—— (2018) *Thinking Without A Bannister*, ed. J. Kohn. New York: Schocken Books.

Arendt, H. and Jaspers, K. (1992) *Correspondence 1926–1979*. New York: Harcourt Brace Jovanovich.

Bernstein, R. J. (1986) "Rethinking the Social and the Political," in R. J. Bernstein, *Philosophical Profiles*, pp. 238–59. Philadelphia: University of Pennsylvania Press.

—— (1996) *Hannah Arendt and the Jewish Question*. Cambridge: Polity.

—— (2016) "Hannah Arendt: Thought-Defying Evil," in R. J. Bernstein, *Pragmatic Encounters*, pp. 140–57. New York: Routledge.

Browning, C. (2003) *Collected Memories: Holocaust History and Postwar Memories*. Madison: University of Wisconsin Press.

Gines, K. T. (2014) *Hannah Arendt and the Negro Question*. Bloomington: Indiana University Press.

Lefort, C. (1988) "Hannah Arendt and the Question of the Political," in C. Lefort, *Democracy and Political Theory*, pp. 45–55. Minneapolis: University of Minnesota Press.

Levi, P. (1996) *Survival in Auschwitz*. New York: Touchstone.

Young-Bruehl, E. (1982) *Hannah Arendt: For Love of the World*. New Haven: Yale University Press.